Timeless Truths

Touching God in Your Daily Living

Brief Devotionals To Begin Your Day

There is an appointed time for everything.
And there is a time for every event under heaven –
Ecclesiastes 3:1 NASB

Patti M. Hummel

Copyright

Timeless Truths

Touching God in Your Daily Living

Brief Devotionals To Begin Your Day

2003 Family Christian Press
All rights reserved.

FAMILY CHRISTIAN PRESS
Grand Rapids, MI 49530

ISBN 1-4041-8485-6

Permission given by the Estate of
Rev. Donald Reed Hummel, Sr. ThM., B.S.
to use portions from his journals

Quotes used by permission from Spiritual Warfare
For Every Christian
c 1990 by Dean Sherman,
Youth With a Mission Publishing.

Permission granted to Patti M. Hummel to
use selected quotes from the Book of Life.

Editing by The Benchmark Group, Nashville, TN
Benchmarkgroup1@aol.com

Layout design by Gale L. Simon, Designer/Illustrator,
The Art Department, Murrieta, CA
gale@theartdepartment.net

Cover design by Karen Phillips

Table of Contents

Table of Contents

There is an appointed time for everything.
And there is a time for every event under heaven –
Ecclesiastes 3:1 NASB

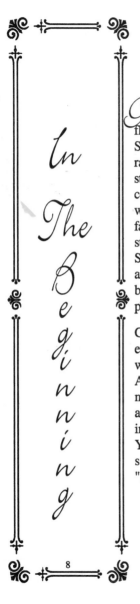

In The Beginning...

$\mathcal{G}$od so wants us to understand that a conflict exists between Satan and Christ. Since the Garden of Eden, it has been raging full-blast in every age and circumstance. This is the basis for all war and conflict, which have occurred, and which will occur. Even of more important is the fact that this is the basis for all of our struggle and trouble in everyday life. Satan constantly attempts to corrupt us and to destroy our fellowship with God, but God is always there, able, and ready to purify us.

Genesis 1-11 shows us the ever-present, ever-ready mercy of God. It would be wise to include His patience, too. Although man was given everything he needed, he wanted more. Sin continued and engulfed the family. It kept spreading and contaminated all of mankind. Yet God continued to be merciful, He sought fallen man and gave every "break" possible.

More Than A Garden

God never changes! We get every chance in the world to repent and receive the blessings of God. He is always ready to aid a seeking heart, in every situation and at any time. God continues to pursue and plead with us as we turn our backs to Him and go our own way. He continually offers Himself in His mercy and justice.

We need to post a guard at the gate of our minds to check the credentials of every thought and every imagination, ready to cast down that which is not true, not righteous, or not of God. If it doesn't belong, out it goes. This is spiritual warfare: being alert to every thought. -- Dean Sherman

Holy Spirit, we need You so desperately to help us to recognize the enemy. Help us to not be afraid to know and understand his ways as well as Yours so we will be best equipped for the battle that has raged since the Garden of Eden. Amen

... for the

battle is

the Lord's...

I Samuel 17:47
NASB

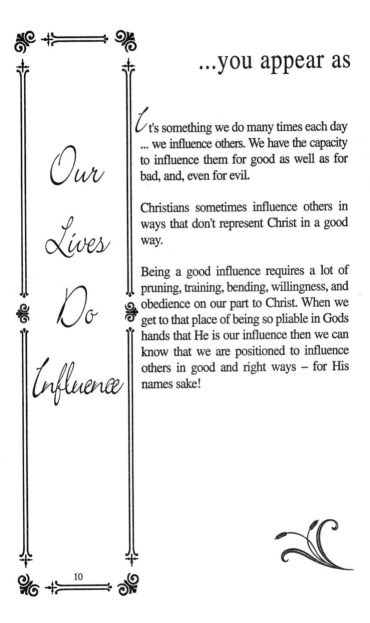

Our

Lives

Do

Influence

It's something we do many times each day ... we influence others. We have the capacity to influence them for good as well as for bad, and, even for evil.

Christians sometimes influence others in ways that don't represent Christ in a good way.

Being a good influence requires a lot of pruning, training, bending, willingness, and obedience on our part to Christ. When we get to that place of being so pliable in Gods hands that He is our influence then we can know that we are positioned to influence others in good and right ways – for His names sake!

lights in the world.

"We cannot affect change whilst we ourselves remain unchanged." – Anon

Lord, God, please help me to be pliable as you work in me to be Your influence to a lost world thereby influencing others with your attributes. Amen

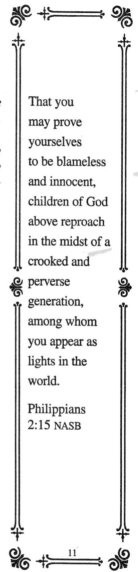

That you may prove yourselves to be blameless and innocent, children of God above reproach in the midst of a crooked and perverse generation, among whom you appear as lights in the world.

Philippians 2:15 NASB

Things Matter, People Matter

Missionary David Brainered spent eight days in the forest asking the Father to descend upon the natives he was called to minister to, who were surrounded by spiritual darkness. When the time came for Mr. Brainered to speak to his audience an interpreter was required. To his dismay Mr. Brainered quickly realized the interpreter was intoxicated. As the missionary spoke and the drunk man interpreted the message, Mr. Brainered became aware of the Holy Spirit moving in power among the people. The message was, in deed, anointed by God. Many came to Jesus Christ as a result of that message that night.

God will use whatever and whomever to get His message out to those who are lost.

time came...

God will not leave us without what we need to do His work. We must, however, be fit vessels for His service by being prepared by Him daily.

Holy God, Your promises are true and You, therefore, cannot leave nor forsake me. Thank You, Father, that in every situation, You are there to strengthen me and to uphold me.
Amen

Do not fear, for I am with you; Do not anxiously look about you, for I am your God. I will strengthen you, surely I will uphold you with My right hand.

Isaiah 41:10
NASB

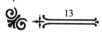

Shut In, But Not Shut Out

$\mathcal{B}$ro. Welsh had been shut in behind four walls for years with a physical ailment that also caused him great pain. His desire was to be "out and about his Fathers business," but he humbly laid or sat looking out his window watching the world move in so many different directions. Often alone, he promised God he would pray. And pray he did. While he was unable to be active physically he prayed that God would be active in the lives of the lost, the lonely, the downtrodden, the infirmed. Mr. Walsh called upon the omnipotent Christ to perform His amazing miracles in the lives of those he knew as well as those he only saw moving outside his window, but never met. Though he couldn't touch, with his own hands, those he prayed for, he was able to ask God, and to trust God, to touch them. Mr. Welsh saw God move mountains in the lives of those he prayed for.

eternal legacy

He left an eternal legacy that will continue for generations because He did not give up, but because he allowed God to use his infirmities to minister to others.

Yes, Lord, since I can pray down Thy mighty doing into the lives I love, shall I longer mourn because I am shut out from doing? What though I cannot do, if Thou, who dost work at my asking can do miracles? So, Lord, though I can do nothing, help me to remember with new joy and hope Thy blessed promise, "If you ask Me anything in My name, I will do it."
– J.H.McConkey

Father God, please make me see that every circumstance in life is an opportunity to minister to this world. Help me to use every moment to bless You.
Amen

If you ask Me

anything

in My name,

I will do it.

John 14:14
NASB

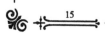

out...

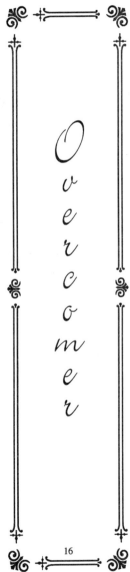

Overcomer

*T*he Hebrew's experience in slavery shows how persecution is used by God to bless Himself and to bless His children. As persecution and seemingly impossible circumstances press us, we can always rely on God's presence. The baby Moses' miraculous preservation is a wonderful example of God's guiding hand in life. When utterly helpless, God remains absolute and constant.

The time Moses was in preparation, compared to his actual time in service is evidence of the importance of preparation. The biggest time of preparation in the life of a Christian is that time spent with God – alone. If we meet God on the mountain, the fighting in the valley is much easier. Much time must be spent before God for even a little time of service.

God knows exactly how much time we need in Boot Camp before we are prepared for battle. We must trust in Him and not allow impatience to get a grip on us. Trust God in all areas, in everything.

# of bondage

God delivered Israel from bondage in Egypt. This very real, historical event is very much like our salvation. When we are saved, we are brought out of bondage. When God led Israel through the Red Sea, we can liken that to our baptism. When God took them into the wilderness, they were to be tested, tempted, attacked, and finally renewed, strengthened, and purified. This also correlates well with the Christian experience. God brought the Israelites into the wilderness to discover whether or not they had what it takes to be the people of GOD. They didn't. God then used the wilderness to produce another generation. Finally after 40 years, a people emerged mature enough, committed enough, and strong enough to be trusted to enter the Promised Land.

Spiritual Warfare for Every Christian
– Dean Sherman

Lord, God, help me to know You in times of persecution, preparation, and when I recognize the very presence of You. Thank You for the balance You have provided to keep me in check at all times when I am committed to Your wondrous work in my life. Amen

For our struggle is not against flesh and blood, but against the rulers, against the powers, against the world forces of this darkness, against the spiritual forces of wickedness in the heavenly places.
Ephesians 6:12
NASB

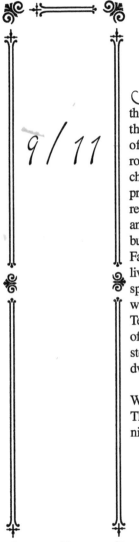

September 11, 2001 will forever live in the hearts and minds of people around the world as the day the United States of America was brutally attacked by terrorists and thousands of lives were lost. A choice was made that day, and for months prior, to take action that would reap horrific results of devastation and chaos to property and human lives. Buildings can be rebuilt, but it takes time to mend wounded souls. Families were displaced for months and lives changed forever as children, parents, spouses, and other relatives and friends were taken from this earth in an instant. Testimonies of those heroic ones who gave of themselves were precious to hear, and stories of how families came together and dwelt with their loss was inspiring to us all.

We never know when our hour will come. The Bible says it comes like a thief in the night. Paul was so committed to Christ

...your new home

that he looked forward, with great hope in his heart, to life after this world passes away. He knew his citizenship was in heaven.

Death might not come to us as an act of terrorism, but it will come. Do you have hope and assurance that death on this earth means moving into your new home in heaven with God? God wants us to live for eternity _ do you?

O God, our help in ages past, Our hope for years to come, Our shelter from the stormy blast, And our eternal home!
– I. Watts

Father God, You sent Your Son to live so He could die so that when we die we can live. Your plan is so perfect. Help us to be prepared and to look forward to death on earth with that blessed hope of spending eternity with You. Amen

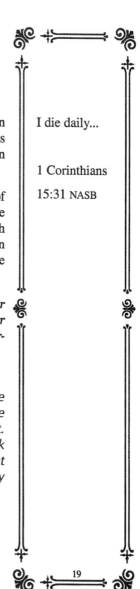

I die daily...

1 Corinthians

15:31 NASB

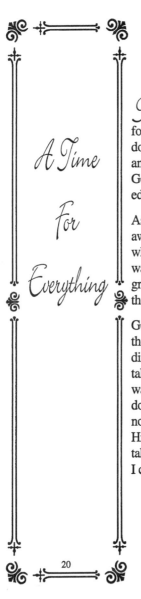

A Time

For

Everything

$\mathcal{T}$he verse says there is an appointed time for everything, but we forget that so easily, don't we? So caught up in the activities and events of life that we forget the plans God has for us and the time He has appointed for those plans to materialize.

As the years pass by I have become more aware of how important it is to wait for what God has for me. No, I don't always wait, for my sinful human nature gets a grip on my emotions and at times I follow them rather than the ways of the Lord.

God, though, is available and ready to pull the reins and get me headed in the right direction again, and again. Sometimes it takes longer than at other times because I want a particular thing so desperately that I don't wait. Those times come when I am not spending time with Christ and trusting Him with my life. Those are the times I take my life back subconsciously thinking I can handle it better than God.

in between

The timeless truth is that He does have a plan and a time to introduce it if we will learn of Him and trust Him with our whole being.

I simply take Him at His word,
I praise Him that my prayer is heard,
And this claim my answer from the
Lord, "I'll take, He undertakes."
I take Thee, blessed Lord…
I give myself to Thee, And Thou,
according to Thy word,
Doest undertake for me.

I Take, He Undertakes
– Rev. A. B. Simpson

Dear Sovereign God, thank You for such love that You planned my life right down from the moment I was born to the split second when I die – and every detail in between. Your love overwhelms me. I am humbled by You, Lord. Thank You that my life, for all time, is appointed by You. Amen

There is an appointed time for everything.

Ecclesiastes 3:1
NASB

No matter

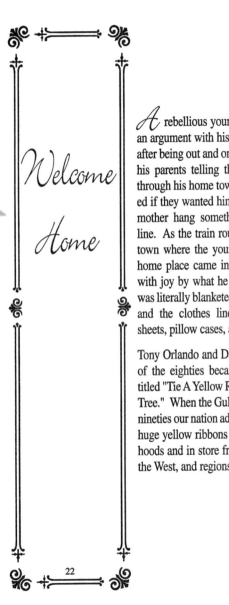

Welcome Home

$\mathcal{A}$ rebellious young man had left home after an argument with his father. Some months later, after being out and on his own, he sent a letter to his parents telling them he would be passing through his home town on the train. He suggested if they wanted him to stop for a visit that his mother hang something white on the clothes line. As the train rounded the bend outside the town where the young man was from and his home place came into view, he was overtaken with joy by what he saw. The little farm house was literally blanketed with white –trees, bushes, and the clothes lines were all covered with sheets, pillow cases, and handkerchiefs.

Tony Orlando and Dawn, a popular singing trio of the eighties became famous for their song titled "Tie A Yellow Ribbon Round The Old Oak Tree." When the Gulf War broke out in the early nineties our nation adopted that song and we saw huge yellow ribbons hanging all over neighborhoods and in store fronts from the East coast to the West, and regions beyond.

what...

Imagine the prodigal son of Scripture, returning home after misappropriating his inherence and having to survive by eating the swine's food. He must have seen the colors of a joyful welcome when his father prepared a feast fit for a king upon his return.

No matter what we have done or how long the separation has been, God is ready to welcome us home. There may not be yellow ribbons on the trees or doors, and there won't be linens waving in the wind from tree branches. There will, though, be heavenly host singing and rejoicing and Christ Himself will be coming toward us with arms outstretched to welcome us home.

We search for peace, although aware that worldly roads lead to despair; But if by faith to Christ we turn, God's grace and truth we'll soon discern. – Anon

Father, we are all prodigals at some time in our lives. I pray that we will always know Your arms of welcome. Amen

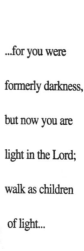

...for you were formerly darkness, but now you are light in the Lord; walk as children of light...

Ephesians 5:8
NASB

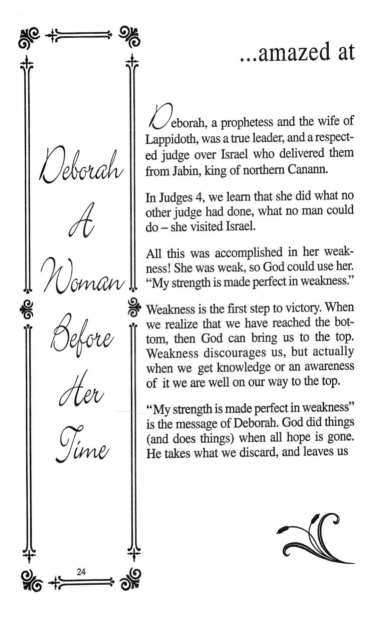

Deborah
A
Woman
Before
Her
Time

Deborah, a prophetess and the wife of Lappidoth, was a true leader, and a respected judge over Israel who delivered them from Jabin, king of northern Canann.

In Judges 4, we learn that she did what no other judge had done, what no man could do – she visited Israel.

All this was accomplished in her weakness! She was weak, so God could use her. "My strength is made perfect in weakness."

Weakness is the first step to victory. When we realize that we have reached the bottom, then God can bring us to the top. Weakness discourages us, but actually when we get knowledge or an awareness of it we are well on our way to the top.

"My strength is made perfect in weakness" is the message of Deborah. God did things (and does things) when all hope is gone. He takes what we discard, and leaves us

what He has done

amazed at what He has done. In actuality, any strength we have is weakness, when we can have His strength.

The life under grace can be a continuos experience of glorious fellowship with the Son of God. It is a miracle life which, like the miracle of creation, is made possible in our dark hearts only by the supernatural light from the face of Christ: "For God who commanded the light to shine out of darkness, hath shined in our hearts, to give light of the knowledge of the glory of God in the face of Jesus Christ."

II Corinthians 4:6 – Roy L. Aldrich

Lord, just as You did in the life of Deborah, I pray Your majesty and grace will be manifested in my life every day. Use me, Dear Father, to make a difference in Your Kingdom here on earth. Amen

"My grace is sufficient for you, for power is perfected in weakness."

II Corinthians 12:9 NASB

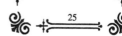

Gideon

A

Visionary

The closer we get to the Lord the more severe are Satan's attacks, as was the case of Gideon. It takes much preparation of us by God for Him to place us in the place He has for us. As we move in relationship toward God, the more power He can bless us with, both to fight off the Foe, and to work for the Lord. Satan can use anyone, for all of us can fall into His clutches. We must continually draw near unto God for deliverance and safety.

The Lord is the guide, so He has the answers to guidance. His way is clear and perfect. God wants disciples, not half hearted followers. He does more where He has full control of a few than where He has partial control of many.

If we are broken before God, submitting to His will, He can shine through us. He doesn't want to merely shine through a crack; He wants us to completely be filled with His light, so that we will be like a beacon to those who still walk in darkness.

draw near unto God

God does all He can to let us be useful to Him, as we submit ourselves, our wills, our past, our present, and our future, to His molding and shaping.

Satan's time of tempting is usually after an ordinance; and the reason is, because then he thinks he shall find us most secure. When we have been at solemn duties, we are apt to think all is done, and we grow remiss, and leave off that zeal and strictness as before; just as a soldier, when after a battle leaves off his armor, not once dreaming, of an enemy. Satan watches his time, and when we least suspect, then he throws in a temptation.
— *Thomas Watson*

God, in heaven, I give myself to You to use for Your work on earth. I realize You might have to crush and mash out a lot of "stuff" I have allowed to become part of my life. Break me, dear God, and use me, I pray. Amen

But the Lord

said to him,

"Surely I will

be with you...

Judges 6:16
NASB

...bu

Average Isaac

He was not really outstanding, as far [as the] Bible space concerning him. He is simpl[y a] connection link, overshadowed by [his] father, Abraham, and his son, Jacob[. It] appears that way, but any person in Go[ds] will is just as important and vital as an[y] one else. Isaac's part, in our eyes, [is] small, but in Gods eyes he played a ve[ry] large part.

We need people who are willing to [be] insignificant in this world, who are will[ing] to do Gods will. An average Isaac in Go[ds] will has done his part and will get [his] reward.

In order to the attaining of all use[ful] knowledge this is most necessa[ry,] that we fear God; we are not quali[fied] to profit by the instructions that a[re] given us unless our minds be possess[ed] with a holy reverence of God, and ev[ery] thought within us be brought into o[be-] dience to Him ... As all our knowle[dge]

in Gods eyes

must take rise from the fear of God, so it must tend to it as its perfection and centre. Those know enough who know how to fear God, who are careful in every thing to please Him and fearful of offending Him in any thing; this is the Alpha and Omega of knowledge. – Matthew Henry

Lord, God, You created all people equally. Help us to love Your creation without judgement. Help us to bless You by looking for You in everyone we know. Amen

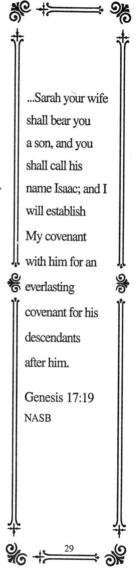

...Sarah your wife shall bear you a son, and you shall call his name Isaac; and I will establish My covenant with him for an everlasting covenant for his descendants after him.

Genesis 17:19
NASB

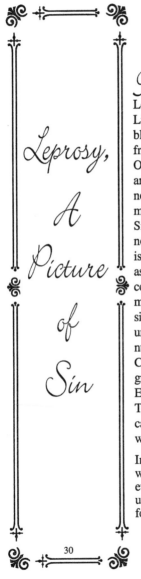

Leprosy, A Picture of Sin

There are many comparisons between Leprosy and sin. Leprosy is a living death. Like Leprosy, a sinner is dead unless the blood has been applied and he is cleansed from his disease. Sin cannot be stopped. Once sin gets a hold on us, and it has, we are doomed within ourselves. We can do nothing, just as a leper can do nothing to make the disease disappear from his body. Sin and leprosy spread freely. Leprosy cannot be hindered and brings sure death. Sin is un-restrainable and brings spiritual death, as well as physical death. Christ has overcome all death. He gave His own life as a payment for ours. Leprosy numbs the senses. So, sin numbs the soul. Conviction of sin is unknown. The more sin abounds, the more numb a soul becomes to the Spirits voice. Children of parents with leprosy have a greater chance of contracting the disease. Every child of man inherits a sinful nature. The leper was forced to stay out of Israel's camp. Today sin keeps us from fellowship with Gods people.

In Bible times a natural cure for leprosy was unknown. So, today, and such will forever be the case, a natural cure for sin is unknown.But Christ is the supernatural cure for both.

finished"

All of the problems of leprosy were cured by God. All of sins problems have been cured by Christ, on the cross. It is up to us to recognize that we are sinners, confess our sins, repent of those sins, and ask Christ Jesus to be our Lord and Savior. The Bible, the Word of God, says that God is faithful and just to forgive our sins. He hung on a cross for each of us and He wants us to come to Him in childlike faith and trust what He has already done for us. The work was completed on Calvary's cross. When Christ said, "It is finished" the Victory was won for all who will accept Him.

Sin is a plague, yea, the greatest and most infectious plague in the world; and yet, ah! how few are there that tremble at it, that keep at a distance from it! – Thomas Brooks

God, You are a God of all compassion. Thank You that You do not cast us out no matter how we look or what sin we have committed. You allow all sinners to come to You in repentance and be saved for all eternity. Thank You for showing us, through Your word, that there is a way of escape.
Amen

No temptation has overtaken you but such as is common to man, and God is faithful, who will not allow you to be tempted beyond what you are able , but with temptation will provide the way of escape also, that you may be able to endure it. I Corinthians 10:13 NASB

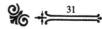

Saved!

$\mathcal{O}$ur salvation is dependent entirely upon Jesus Christ and His shed blood. Although our salvation is dependent entirely upon Him, we don't possess it until we believe and accept His finished work. We cannot please God without faith.

Gods own infallible Word tells us once saved we are saved eternally. "Believe on the Lord Jesus Christ, and thou shalt be saved. Him that cometh unto me, I will in no wise cast out. If we confess our sins He is faithful and just to forgive us our sins and to cleanse us from all unrighteousness. But as many as received Him to them gave He the power to become the sons of God; even to them that believe on His name. Now unto Him that is able to keep you from falling and to present you faultless before His presence with exceeding joy. I am the way, the truth, and the life; no man cometh unto the Father but by Me."

God made the world and everything that is on the earth. God is able, and the only one who is able, to not only be the creator, but the Savior. He sent His only Son to the earth to live as a man do and die so that we can have life eternal. The Bible tells us that we have all sinned and we all stand in need of Him. There is nothing we

...of God

can do or say that can open the gates of heaven for our entry. There is only one way to become a Christian... a child of God, a family member in the Kingdom... that is to confess our sins, repent, ask the Lord Jesus Christ to forgive our sins, and accept Him as our Lord and Savior. He has already done the work! Salvation is a gift! There is never a time Christ will not hear the prayer of a sinner who confesses, repents, and ask for Him to have control of their life.

The very moment we tell Christ we accept His gift we receive salvation, eternally. It is then we do good works, not to retain our salvation, but to be a blessing to the Lord and His Kingdom here on earth, and to bring blessing when we enter heaven.

Jesus loves me! He who died Heaven's gate to open wide" He will wash away my sin, Let His little children in. Yes, Jesus loves me! Yes, Jesus loves me! Yes, Jesus loves me! The Bible tells me so.
– William B. Bradbury

God, Your gift of Your only Son so we may come to salvation is the ultimate gift. Salvation is forever and for that, we are grateful to You. Amen

No temptation has overtaken you but such as is common to man, and God is faithful, who will not allow you to be tempted beyond what you are able , but with temptation will provide the way of escape also, that you may be able to endure it. I Corinthians 10:13 NASB

My

Shepherd

$\mathcal{U}$f you spent time in church as a child you probably memorized the 23rd Psalm as I did. Nonetheless, not until a few years ago did I actually sit at my Shepherds feet and meditate on this Psalm of David. It took days to get through each morsel of this tiny chapter. I wept for hours as the Holy Spirit taught me and loved me through it. An unforgettable time spiritually, but one that created such a change in me that I was completely humbled by what I thought I already knew. What had seemed so easy to say was now a living part of me.

The Lord is My Shepherd! The LORD IS MY SHEPHERD! THE LORD (GOD) IS MY SHEPHERD! That alone is enough to bring us to our knees. He loves us so much that He is willing to Shepherd us throughout our lives. He, as our Shepherd, is concerned

living part of me.

about us so much that He watches over us, blesses us, loves us, and even laid His life down for ours. He sees value and worth in us and He encourages us to be strong, mighty, like Him, and to spend eternity with Him in Paradise. Imagine that, He wants us in Paradise – with HIM! How overwhelming to think of God, who is MY SHEPHERD. MY SHEPHERD! All He asks of us is that we follow! Follow Him, the Good Shepherd.

Dear Shepherd, thank You for all Your wonderful attributes that You shower me with daily. I am so grateful that You are MY SHEPHERD. I pray that I will follow You and learn from You in obedience to You so my life will Honor You. Amen

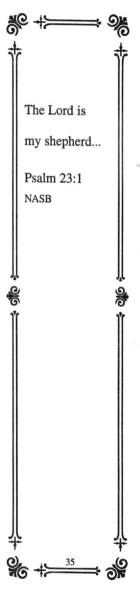

The Lord is

my shepherd...

Psalm 23:1

NASB

His

Will

Alone

The issue is not that I am now to determine Gods ultimate will, but only His present will." – D.R. Hummel, Sr.

We literally must use our own will to turn our hearts to decisions of Gods will. Not so easy for us when the world with all its excitement, ease, and momentary thrills, pulls us in a different direction. Of course, the world rarely, if ever, shows the true or whole picture. Most often the end of that direction is distorted or not in view at all.

The important thing is not our own feelings, desires, reasons, but rather, HIS WILL, ALONE! We must obey HIM – we must seek to know HIS WILL, ALONE! It is okay to ask Christ for His surety; we are fallible human beings and He knows our insecurities and weaknesses. He is pleased when we talk to Him about things that concern us or those things we are insecure about.

# of surrender

When we seek His will and objectively accept it, no matter what our present experience, there is freedom and surety in that decision. Everything is then HIS responsibility, as it should be. Once we are utterly open to God in our need, we can then love, enjoy, and embrace His will easily – then comes freedom in Christ. Yes, it takes forgetting self and becoming totally dependent upon HIM. Faith is required to get to this place of surrender, but as we seek Him, even for the faith necessary, He is ready to release to us all we need to be what He wants us to be.

Lord, make me the mighty one You desire me to be. Help me when I am weak. Guide me when I start to move in wrong directions. Thank you for providing all I need to live out the plans You have for my life. Amen

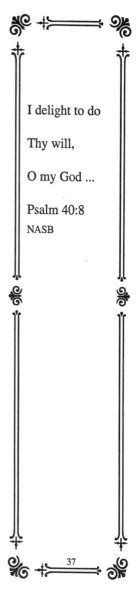

I delight to do

Thy will,

O my God ...

Psalm 40:8
NASB

A Lesson Taught, A Lesson Learned

...a view no other

Training children in the ways of the Lord can be a real chore especially when we, adults, are learning the same lessons. Demanding our rights is a huge issue for most people and can manifest itself in some undesirable ways. Kids are no different. They want what they think they should have. My children were on the brink of taking on some pretty awful attitudes and I knew I had to intervene. A summer vacation seemed like a great time to help them understand the importance of waiting patiently for what God had for them. Leaving an amusement park at closing, after a long day in the hot Florida sun, was the last place I would have considered a lesson to be learned. There I stood in line with my three young children, drained and tired from the days activities and heat, waiting for the last tram to take us to our hotel and some much needed rest. Suddenly, and to our utter surprise, a young couple pushed their way in front of us and took the last available seats. All I could say as my kids looked up at me was that God would provide. Just as quickly, the conductor, who had witnessed the scene, came from the front car and offered us a ride in the engine car. Once in the nose of that electronic marvel, with a view no other passenger could imagine, one of my sons spoke up and said, "Jesus blessed us because we waited patiently and we did not push that rude couple out of our way." Okay, he did call them rude, but I think he realized a valuable lesson that night.

passenger could imagine

When we do what is right and do not demand what we think are our rights, God will take care of us. When God does a thing, there are no limits to the way He can and will bless His children. I would have called a cab and the four of us would have been cramped into the back seat all the way back to our hotel, but God gave my kids the ride of their life, and the conductor told them things about the engine and pointed out things along the way that we would have missed had we been in a cab or any other seat on the tram. What lessons we can enjoy when we allow Him to be God in our lives. Humility does not mean we are wimps, it does mean respect and obedience.

A truly humble man is sensible of his natural distance from God; of his dependence of Him; of the insufficiency of his own power and wisdom; and that it is by Gods power that he is upheld and provided for, and that he needs God's wisdom to lead and guide him, and His might to enable him to do what he ought to do for Him.

– Jonathan Edwards

Dear Lord, it would be so natural, and so right in the eyes of the world, to demand a certain place, a particular position, and my rights! Help me to allow You to humble me to the place of total dependence upon You for what is Your best for me. Amen

For the Lord loves justice, And does not forsake His Godly ones. They are preserved forever.

Psalm 37:28
NASB

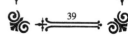

Never Without A Helper

$\mathcal{T}$here are those things we recognize as those only God is able to do and all that is required of us is to pray. Hope springs forth when we ask God to work in ways only He can. God calls each of us to some place of service yet we must still ask Him to guide us, to protect us, to provide for us, and to do His work within the area He called us to. All we do must first be covered with prayer never forgetting that it is God who ultimately does all the spiritual work – no matter how actively involved we are.

Without the work of the Holy Spirit our labors are in vain. Perhaps that is the reason so many fail in the great commission – a call not covered in prayer is just that – a call! A call covered in prayer is becomes the powerful working of the Holy Spirit to do the work of the Father, the work we cannot do without Him.

impossible things

When you do what is right, without tiring of it, God takes care of the impossible things.

– Dr. Charles R. Swindoll

Holy Spirit, I need You to be actively at work in my life so that I will walk where I am to walk and do what I am to do, leaving Your work for You to do, as I pray for Your will to be done.
Amen

And I will ask the Father, and He will give you another Helper that He may be with you forever.

John 14:17
NASB

I'm standing on

I'm standing on the promises of God.
-R. Kelso Carter

As faith based missionaries trips back to the US mainland were costly no matter why or when we made them. A necessary trip came up one year the week before Christmas. My sons had out grown all the winter clothes taken with us when we went to the South Pacific. Once we landed in California we were greeted by the pastor who used our car while we were on the field and we were quickly on our way to Georgia. The temperature steadily decreased and our bodies, now acclimated to the tropics, could not endure the cold. We prayed that God would lead us to a place to purchase coats, sweater, gloves, and hats at deep discounts. I tried to impress upon my teenage sons that the trip home would be our Christmas and there wasn't even money to purchase a tree. There were too many necessary items, like warm clothing, that had to be purchased. My oldest son, who had recently experienced a bit of a spiritual revival in his own life, kept reassuring his brother and me that God would provide a tree for us ... "He'll do it, Mom, God will do it."

We continued to pray for a shopping place in the Arizona flats when suddenly, in the middle of no where, appeared a billboard advertising "BIG SALES" on winter clothes. Upon entry we found

the promises of God.

everything we needed and God blessed us with lovely and stylish clothes. The total came to just under $51.00. When the cashier handed me the receipt she said, "Now, don't forget your tree!" To our amazement, any purchase over $50 allowed the shopper to go to a simi parked outside the store and pick out a Christmas tree ... already trimmed! We loaded that tree in to the back of that station wagon and enjoyed the fragrance of the evergreen for the next 1,800 miles as we sang Christmas carols and hymns thanking God. It took the faith of a young boy to realize Gods grand scale of blessings to His children that Christmas. Those same blessings are waiting for every Christian to enjoy, but we must trust Him. God who gave His only son at Christmas more than 2000 years before, so we may spend eternity with Him, is the same God who provided that Christmas tree to a young missionary boy. The fragrance of Christmas trees reminds me every year of those two amazing Christmases.

Jesus, You came to earth to be our Savior and that is the greatest gift of all, but You continue to give in the simplest of ways. You are such a loving God. Help us, Your children to learn from You, how to recognize the need to give, when to give, what to give, and to do it all so that You will be glorified. Amen

Every good thing bestowed andevery perfect gift is from above coming down from the Father of lights, with whom there is no variation, or shifting shadow.

James 1:17
NASB

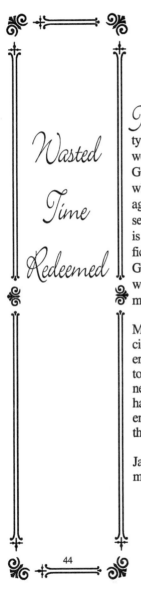

Wasted Time Redeemed

The trial, adversity, blessing, and prosperity in Jacob's life exemplify that "all things work together for good to them that love God" as Romans 8:28 tells us. No matter what may come our way, nor how much against us circumstances or people may seem, everything works for our good. God is continually at work in our lives. Self-sufficiency is our greatest sin. We must see Gods glory, and then we will see our own weakness and our need for Gods grace. We must daily see Gods grace-sufficiency.

Many times in the existence of self-sufficiency God has to make unusable or inoperative our own self to make room for Him to work. He has to show us how much we need Him, how little we are on our own. We have to go through times of trouble, and endure pain at times in order to recognize the real source of our strength.

Jacob wasted twenty years. We, too, waste much time; all of the time we spend in our

the promises of God.

own strength, all of the time we spend depending upon the natural is wasted time, in a sense. We struggle and struggle trying to accomplish something, when all we have to do is turn to God who is always ready to work out everything in the best way possible.

.. if believers decay in their first love, or in some other grace, yet another grace may grow and increase, such as humility, their brokenheartedness; they sometimes seem not to grow in the branches when they may grow at the root; upon a check grace breaks out more, as we say, after a hard winter there usually follows a glorious spring. – Richard Sibbes

Father, forgive me, please, for wasting valuable time here on earth. Help me to know You so well that I will recognize the trials I endure as well as every good experience are for my growth in grace as a Christian. Thank You, for examples in Your Word that help me to walk down right paths. Amen

Every good thing bestowed and every perfect gift is from above coming down from the Father of lights, with whom there is no variation, or shifting shadow.

James 1:17
NASB

Moving

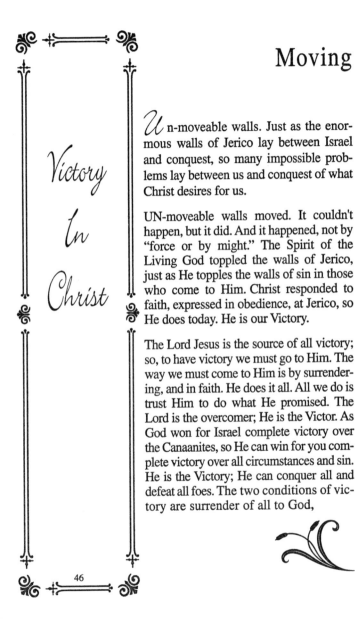

Victory In Christ

𝒰 n-moveable walls. Just as the enormous walls of Jerico lay between Israel and conquest, so many impossible problems lay between us and conquest of what Christ desires for us.

UN-moveable walls moved. It couldn't happen, but it did. And it happened, not by "force or by might." The Spirit of the Living God toppled the walls of Jerico, just as He topples the walls of sin in those who come to Him. Christ responded to faith, expressed in obedience, at Jerico, so He does today. He is our Victory.

The Lord Jesus is the source of all victory; so, to have victory we must go to Him. The way we must come to Him is by surrendering, and in faith. He does it all. All we do is trust Him to do what He promised. The Lord is the overcomer; He is the Victor. As God won for Israel complete victory over the Canaanites, so He can win for you complete victory over all circumstances and sin. He is the Victory; He can conquer all and defeat all foes. The two conditions of victory are surrender of all to God,

walls

including every circumstance in and every phase of our lives, and faith in God to deliver us from all sin into full victory. He has the answer to every problem.

Encamped along the hills of light,
Ye Christian soldiers rise,
And press the battle ere the night
Shall veil the glowing skies.
Against the foe
In vales below,
Let all our strength be hurled;
Faith is the victory, we know,
That overcomes the world.
His banner over us is love,
Our sword the Word of God;
We tread the road the saints above
With shouts of triumph trod.
By faith they, like a whirlwind's breath,
Swept on o'er every field,
The faith by which they conquered death
Is still out shining shield.
– Ira D. Sankey

Dear Lord, I am weak, and without You I would stay defeated. But You are my God and Father, and I look to You to move the walls in my life. Amen

Thine, O Lord,

is the greatness

and the power

and the glory

and the victory

and the

majesty...

I Chronicles

29:11 NASB

He is just a

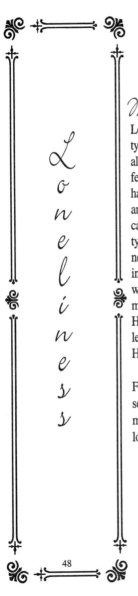

L o n e l i n e s s

$\mathcal{M}$ost people are cognizant of loneliness. Loneliness affects us with overwhelming intensity at some time in our lives. It is no fun to feel alone. Yet, most of us can feel very alone for a few moments and just as quickly realize that we have friends and family members who love us and who care about us with deep emotion. We can tune our hearts and minds back to the reality and comfort of feeling close and of being needed and cared for. Christians have a deep and intimate hope of spending eternity with God, who is love, which causes the loneliness to fade more quickly and not return as often. We know He is with us now and we know He will never leave nor forsake us because He promised that He would not.

For many, times of loneliness are empty and may seem almost constant. Even though there may be moments of feeling needed, cared for, and even loved, without a lasting, eternal hope in the

prayer away...

person of Jesus Christ, the loneliness returns and casts a shadow over life that can be haunting and debilitating. At this point it begins to affect every aspect of life and every relationship we have.

Jesus is the answer to loneliness! He has promised to be our burden barer and He said He will wipe away all our tears. Jesus wants us to find joy and happiness in Him. By doing so we can become acquainted with His peace, which takes the sting out of certain times of loneliness. He puts contentment in the place of fear of being alone. He is available. He is just a prayer away.

Jesus: It is so comforting to know that You are always with me. No matter how afraid I am or under what circumstances I am in, You will not forsake me. Thank You Lord, for Your Word that is reassuring to me. Amen.

And surely I am with you always, to the very end of the age.

Matthew 28:20
NIV

exceeding

Saying Goodbye

$\mathcal{W}$atching a loved one pass from this life into glory is not easy. There is a pain so deep that words cannot give a true impression of it. Nothing anyone says, though given in sincere sympathy, can console the heart. Realizing that we will never see or talk with the one who had been so dear to us is a gut-wrenching agony to deal with. In the days after the funeral, we find ourselves reaching for the phone to call our friend, we want to share some part of our life with them. Then, and again, we are reminded that they are not where they were just a week ago ... they are no longer available to us.

We rejoice that they are with Christ in heaven and loving Him and His creation in ways that we will hope for until He calls us home. We miss our friend, our loved one. No one on earth can take the place of the one who just moved on up!

abundantly above all

God wants us to call on Him in these times of mourning. He bore our sorrows and He is acquainted with grief. He is also the one, the only one who is able to do exceeding abundantly above all that we can ask or even imagine. We are so blessed to have a heavenly Father who loves us so much that He bears our sorrows.

Dear Father: Thank You for Your tender heart toward Your children who mourn. Thank You for loving us so much that You gave us tears to cleanse some of the pain. Tell my friend and loved one how happy I am they are with You, able to enjoy all You have prepared there for them. And, Lord, tell them how much I look forward to seeing them again, when You call me to my heavenly home. Amen

... to Him who is able to do exceeding abundantly beyond all that we ask or think, according to the power that works within us...

Ephesians 3:20
NASB

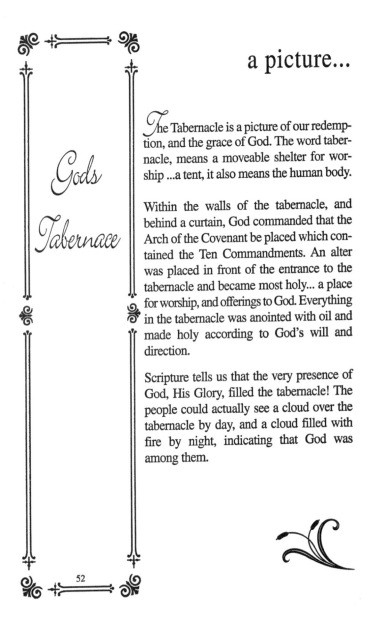

a picture...

God's Tabernacle

The Tabernacle is a picture of our redemption, and the grace of God. The word tabernacle, means a moveable shelter for worship ...a tent, it also means the human body.

Within the walls of the tabernacle, and behind a curtain, God commanded that the Arch of the Covenant be placed which contained the Ten Commandments. An alter was placed in front of the entrance to the tabernacle and became most holy... a place for worship, and offerings to God. Everything in the tabernacle was anointed with oil and made holy according to God's will and direction.

Scripture tells us that the very presence of God, His Glory, filled the tabernacle! The people could actually see a cloud over the tabernacle by day, and a cloud filled with fire by night, indicating that God was among them.

# of our redemption

As children of God, traveling through life, we can become that "moveable shelter for worship". Our Father has placed his Covenant in our hearts, and His Spirit dwells within us!

Through His grace we are cleansed of our sin and our lives become a sweet offering.

Holy Spirit, all divine
Dwell within this heart of mine;
Cast down every idol throne,
Reign supreme, and reign alone
– Andrew Reed

God, You are holy. I pray as You have made provision for Your children to enter into a covenant relationship with You, that our worship will honor You as Holiness. Amen

For I am

the Lord your

God.

Consecrate

yourselves

therefore,

and be holy;

for I am holy.

Leviticus 11:44

NASB

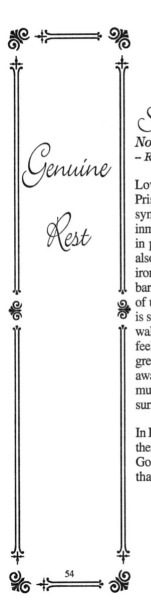

ACTION

Genuine Rest

$\mathcal{S}$tone walls do not a prison make,
Nor iron bars a cage."
-- Richard Lovelace

Lovelace wrote in "To Althea from Prison Song" while serving for Royalist sympathies. He understood that many inmates though surrounded by bars, are not in prison, they are FREE – internally. He also understood that many are without the iron bars, but are under such bondage that bars of hopelessness surround them. Most of us experience a time when the pressure is so great that we feel being behind prison walls would be a better place to be. That feeling of imprisonment, no matter how great the trial, will pass and we can move away from that time, whereas the prisoner must continue to endure the bars that do surround him.

In Hebrews 4:9 we are told, "There remains therefore a Sabboth rest for the people of God" NASB. What an important reminder that when we can feel the imaginary bars

required

closing in all around us that God has made a place of rest when we are "diligent to enter that rest."

ACTION is required so we can enter into that rest. Faith is that action. The same rest is available to the real prisoner. He or she can enter into that rest by making a conscious decision to do so. God can penetrate bars as well as hearts. We must allow Him a place to set up residence in our hearts, as Lord and Savior, so He can work His will. God can and will bring peace that passes all understanding and peace that will make a prisoner see how far he has come rather than dwelling on how much longer he has to be there.

Father God, I pray for Your peaceful rest to enter the hearts of prisoners. Help them to know that You are the same God inside and outside the bars that separate them from the outside world. I pray, too, that You, dear God, will remind me to pray for and care for the prisoner. Amen

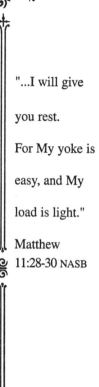

"...I will give you rest. For My yoke is easy, and My load is light."

Matthew 11:28-30 NASB

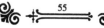

Keeping

Doubt

Doubts visit the Christian daily. Because of this overwhelming emotion we must know who we are in Christ. We must know Christ, and, yes, we must know who Satan is so we can recognize his work.

Peter was oblivious to the huge waves that surrounded him as he heard the Lord tell him to step out of the boat and walk on the water. Once he began to doubt, he saw – instantly – all the dangers around him as he took his eyes off Christ. Doubt caused him to sink. Doubt will do the same thing for us ... cause us to sink. Keeping our eyes on Jesus through faith is what we need to do so we can make it to every shore in life.

our eyes on Jesus

In the bitter waves of woe
Beaten and tossed about
By the sullen winds that blow
From desolate shores of doubt,
Where the anchors that faith
has cast
Are dragging in the gale,
I am quietly holding fast
To the things that cannot fail.
And fierce though the fiends may
fight,
And long though the angels hide,
I know that truth and right
Have the universe on their side;
And that somewhere beyond
the stars
Is a love that is better than fate.
When the night unlocks her bars
I shall see Him -- and I will wait.
-- Washington Gladden

Help me, Lord, to have faith that is
dead to doubts, dumb to discourage-
ments, and blind to impossibilities.
Amen

... if you

have faith,

and do not

doubt...

it shall happen.

Matthew 21:21
NASB

Come

Follow The Lead

*F*ormer President Eisenhower used to explain leadership by laying a string on a table and pulling it. As he pulled it, the string always followed. Then he would stop and push on the string and it would lay motionless until he pushed it again. Pushing a person requires another push each time you want a thing accomplished. A good leader sets examples by leading and not by pushing.

Christ is the example for the Christian life. Problem is, so often we don't follow His leadership because we are so busy being pushed around, one push at a time by our own desires, the enemy, the world, etc. It is our choice to follow our leader or we may find ourselves being pushed right out of His blessings and goodness.

our eyes on Jesus

Sweetly, Lord, have we heard Thee calling, Come follow me! And we see where Thy footprints falling, lead us to Thee.

Dear Shepherd, Your leading is the only way for me to go. You lead me in the paths of righteousness. Help me to always want to follow You. Amen

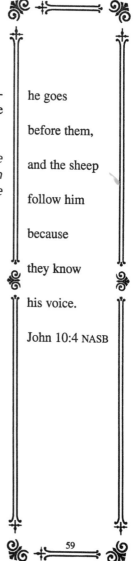

he goes

before them,

and the sheep

follow him

because

they know

his voice.

John 10:4 NASB

The Prize

$\mathcal{G}$rowing up very poor in the rural south brought with it many hard lessons. There were many fun times and interesting things to be learned as well, and those lessons came in a plethora of ways. The farmer neighbor a few pastures behind us needed help picking his cotton. My parents agreed that we could assist him and he would pay us for our labor. The night before the big day of picking came, my sister and I sat flipping through a Sears & Roebuck catalog choosing all the items we would buy with our new found income. The next day we struggled to hoist the bags over our shoulders while picking as fast and hard as we could, all-the-while dreaming of the grand shopping trip that would surely come. Yet, by the days end we were not only exhausted, but had quickly become disillusioned about the benefits of picking cotton for a living... for all our intense labor, we only made fifteen cents each.

Not too unlike adult Christians, myself included, who make plans and dream dreams... leaving God completely out of

picking cotton

the picture. Yet, it is Christ who promised to supply all our needs. He wants us to work, but He wants us to do what His will is for our work. I often think of that day picking cotton and remember that even then I had no desire to pick cotton for a living. I also recall how greedy I was and have since asked God to help me to trust Him for my supply.

Onward and upward your course plan today, Seeking new heights as you walk Jesus' way; Heeding not past failures, but strive for the prize, Aiming for goals fit for His holy eyes.

- Brandt

Lord, God, help me to look to You for what I need. Realizing You have work for me to do here on earth, but following what Your will is for that work. *Amen*

And my God shall supply all your needs according to His riches in glory in Christ Jesus.

Philippians 4:19 NASB

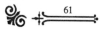

Everything

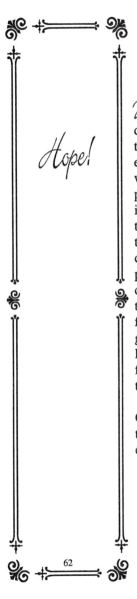

Hope!

$\mathscr{M}$artin Luther said, "Everything that is done in the world is done by hope." So true. Think about it — we do hope in everything. We hope for a good day, time with our families, great jobs with timely pay increases, and we hope for the best in everything. Some also hope for things that aren't necessary or even good for them. Depending on our age, or our circumstances, one could hope the kid picking on him in school would fall down and break his leg, or the company that recently laid you off would be forced to file bankruptcy. We hope for good and bad. What are you hoping for in life? In eternity? Is your hope securely focused on a Holy God? Or are you looking to man made gods – idols?

God is able to control everything relating to a man and all the influences that are directed toward Him.

that is done

Wishful thinking is past tense. Hope is future tense. When our hope is in Christ, our future is secure. – DRH

Father, help my heart to turn toward You in faith, and dependence, and hope. Amen

Which is Christ in you, the hope of glory.

Colossians 1:27
NASB

The Grace of God

A shamefaced employee was summoned to the office of the senior partner to hear his doom. The least that he could expect was a blistering dismissal: he might be sent to prison for years. The old man called his name and asked him if he were guilty. The clerk stammered that he had no defense. "I shall not send you to prison," said the old man. "If I take you back, can I trust you?" When the surprised and broken clerk had given assurance and was about to leave, the senior partner continued: "You are the second man who has fallen and been pardoned, in this business. I was the first. What you have done, I did. The mercy you have received, I received. It is only the grace of God that can keep us both". – Anon

what...

In the model prayer, which we refer to as The Lord's Prayer, Christ tells us to forgive, not forgetting how we have been forgiven. There are crimes that must be punished, and discipline has to take place in all of our lives or there would be total chaos in the world. However, God also wants us to forgive others in His love and by His grace. It is only through Him that we can forgive and love those who have harmed us, taken valuable items from us, or hurt the ones we love. Once saved we are then equipped with the Holy Spirit and can call upon Him to help us forgive and love those we could not love and forgive without Christ.

Father, You have taught us how to love and how to forgive. Help us to recall these lessons each time we are faced with the painful things people can do to us. Help us to remember that we are dead to sin and can trust You to help us be Christlike in our lives. Amen

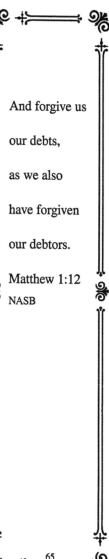

And forgive us our debts, as we also have forgiven our debtors.

Matthew 1:12 NASB

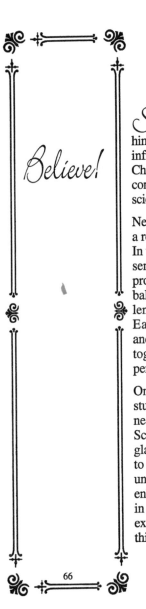

Believe!

Sir Isaac Newton had a friend who, like himself, was a great scientist; but he was an infidel, while Newton was a devout Christian. They often discussed their views concerning God, as their mutual interest in science drew them much together.

Newton had a skillful mechanic make him a replica of our solar system in miniature. In the center was a large gilded ball representing the sun, and revolving in their proper order around them were small balls fixed on the ends of arms of varying lengths, representing Mercury, Venus, Earth, Mars, Jupiter, Saturn, Uranus, and Neptune. These balls were so geared together by cogs and belts as to move in perfect harmony when turned by a crank.

One day, as Newton sat reading in his study with his mechanism on a large table near him, his infidel friend stepped in. Scientist that he was, he recognized at a glance what was before him. Stepping up to it, he slowly turned the crank, and with undisguised admiration watched the heavenly bodies all move in their relative speed in their orbits. Standing off a few feet, he exclaimed, "My! What an exquisite thing this is! Who made it?"

made it?"

Without looking up from his book, Newton answered, "Nobody!"

Quickly turning to Newton, the infidel said, "Evidently you did not understand my question. I asked who made this?" Looking up now, Newton solemnly assured him that nobody made it, but that the aggregation of matter so much admired had just happened to assume the form it was in.

But the astonished infidel replied with some heat, "You must think I am a fool! Of course somebody made it, and he is a genius, and I'd like to know who he is."

Laying his book aside, Newton arose and laid a hand on his friend's shoulder. "This thing is but a puny imitation of a much grander system whose laws you know, and I am not able to connivance you that this mere toy is without a designer and maker; yet you profess to believe that the great original form which the design is taken has come into being without either designer or maker! Now tell me by what sort of reasoning do you reach such an incongruous conclusion?" The infidel was at once convinced and became a firm believer that "Jehovah, He is the God."

–Anon

Yes, Lord;

I have believed

that You are

the Christ...

John 11:27

NASB

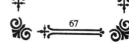

C o m m u n i c a t i o n

Guarantees

Balance

Our hearts tend to move up and down in our relationship with Christ. This perplexes most of us to the point of questioning God about our salvation. We often have an attitude of dependence in life situations rather than communion alone with Christ. Fellowship with a seasoned Christian aids us as we see how experienced victory draws us to communion. Often, accompanying a period of defeat is a paralleled time of devotion with God. God knows how to bring balance to our lives, Communion and faith go hand-in-hand.

How thrilling to know that God fully understands mood swings. He is a God of order and wants us to have lives that are balanced. Balance can only come to the life of a Christian when communion with Christ is foundational. He wants our time and attention in sweet communion with us.

in hand

If we could push ajar the gates of life,
And stand within, and all God's working
see,
We might interpret all this doubt and
strife,
And for each mystery could find a key.
But not today.
Then be content, poor heart;
Gods plans, like lilies pure and white,
unfold.
We must not tear the closed shut leaves
apart –
Time will reveal the calyxes of gold.
And if, through patient toil, we reach the
land
Where tired feet, with sandals loosed,
may rest,
When we shall clearly know and under-
stand, I think that we shall say,
"God knew best." Anon

Lord, You are a God of order and it is
our desire to commune with You and
enjoy that same sense of order and bal-
ance in our own lives. Thank You for
showing us how to achieve these areas
in our lives. Amen

And do not be conformed to this world, but be transformed by the renewing of your minds, that you may prove what the will of God is, that which is good and acceptable and perfect.

Romans 12:2

NASB

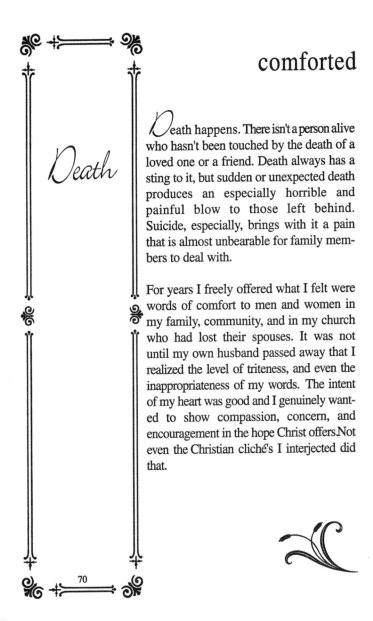

comforted

Death

*D*eath happens. There isn't a person alive who hasn't been touched by the death of a loved one or a friend. Death always has a sting to it, but sudden or unexpected death produces an especially horrible and painful blow to those left behind. Suicide, especially, brings with it a pain that is almost unbearable for family members to deal with.

For years I freely offered what I felt were words of comfort to men and women in my family, community, and in my church who had lost their spouses. It was not until my own husband passed away that I realized the level of triteness, and even the inappropriateness of my words. The intent of my heart was good and I genuinely wanted to show compassion, concern, and encouragement in the hope Christ offers.Not even the Christian cliché's I interjected did that.

by God

God wants us to be available to those who are grieving. The Bible teaches us in the first chapter of II Corinthians that, "God is all comfort." God is our example to emulate "so that we may be able to comfort those who are in any affliction with the comfort with which we ourselves are comforted by God."

Jesus shares your worries and cares, You'll never be left all alone; For He stands beside you to comfort and guide you, He always looks out for His own.
– Brandt

God, of all comfort, we need You to show us how to comfort those we love when they grieve. Help us to speak Your words in tenderness thereby opening the door for them to reach out when they are ready.
Amen

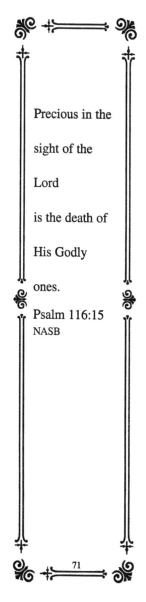

Precious in the sight of the Lord is the death of His Godly ones.

Psalm 116:15
NASB

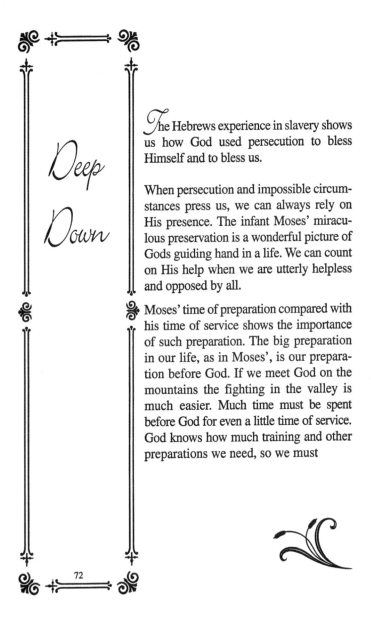

Deep Down

The Hebrews experience in slavery shows us how God used persecution to bless Himself and to bless us.

When persecution and impossible circumstances press us, we can always rely on His presence. The infant Moses' miraculous preservation is a wonderful picture of Gods guiding hand in a life. We can count on His help when we are utterly helpless and opposed by all.

Moses' time of preparation compared with his time of service shows the importance of such preparation. The big preparation in our life, as in Moses', is our preparation before God. If we meet God on the mountains the fighting in the valley is much easier. Much time must be spent before God for even a little time of service. God knows how much training and other preparations we need, so we must

in every place.

trust in Him and not let impatience get a stronghold. Trust God in all things … including the valleys that will be a part of the Christian life. He is on the mountain tops, but He is deep in the valleys with and for us when we are there. He can be trusted in every place.

There is no greater witness in the world than that of a Christian who endures, who truly exults in and overcomes everything the world and the devil can throw at him. Making these things work for us and not against us is real spiritual warfare. – Dean Sherman

Lord, God, Jehovah, You show Your greatness to Your children by teaching and providing and protecting us. We adore You. Help us to meet You so we can be prepared for life! Amen

When you pass through the waters, I will be with you; And through the rivers, they will not overflow you. When you walk through the fire, you will not be scorched, nor will the flame burn you, For I am the Lord, your God, the Holy one of Israel, your Savior

Isaiah 43:2-3
NASB

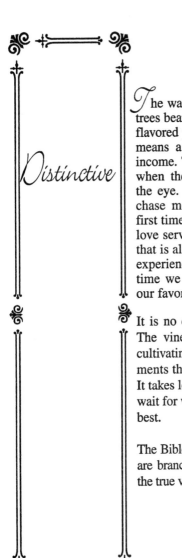

I am

Distinctive

$\mathcal{T}$he wait is always worth it when fruit trees bear an abundance of luscious full-flavored plump fruit. Farmers know this means a yield that will bring a hefty income. The grocer is able to sell more when the presentation is appealing to the eye. Customers will return to purchase more of what they enjoyed the first time when the taste is good. Moms love serving their families healthy fruit that is also flavorful, and our taste buds experience a wonderful sensation each time we bite into a succulent piece of our favorite fruit.

It is no easy task to raise quality fruit. The vine or tree requires tending and cultivating while considering all the elements that could potentially destroy it. It takes long hours and there is a lengthy wait for what we consider the best of the best.

The Bible tells us that we, Gods children, are branches that also require tending by the true vinedresser, who is God. He will

the vine

nourish us and help us to grow to be mighty men and women in Christ if we will submit to the necessary cultivation. John 15:5 reminds us, "I am the vine, you are the branches; he who abides in Me, and I in him, he bears much fruit ..."

Make sure your fruit is useful, not useless. -Anon

God, I pray that I will bear fruit that is flavorful. That my life will be succulent and pleasurable to fellow believers and to the lost of the world. Amen

The fruit of the righteous is a tree of life....

Proverbs 11:31
NASB

When

Fading Scars

At some time in our lives we acquire scars that we can see for the rest of our lives. Being right handed has allowed for more injuries to my right hand and arm that are visible. I have two scars on my arm that came from removing a cookie sheet from a hot oven with a wet oven MIT. The heat was transferred through the MIT and when my fingers felt the intense heat, I reacted, and bounced the cookie sheet against my arm... twice! These scars are permanent. It took weeks for my arm to heal from the infection caused by the burns. These two distinct scars have not faded over the years. However, I have other scars on that hand and arm that have either faded almost to obscurity or seem to be headed in that directions.

God saves...

When Christ saves us we often have many scars from a life in sin that have to heal. Some of our scars stem from abuse, dysfunction, or trauma. Although we are saved and have assurance of eternity with Christ, there are areas that might take a long time to heal. Circumstances must still be dealt with and the consequences of past sins often have to be accounted for. When God saves, He blots out all our transgressions, but we live on earth and we must be responsible to deal with issues until they also fade away.

Just like scars on our bodies that fade as the years pass by, so will the scars of our past pass and be just that, the past! – *PMH*

God, my Father, help me to move forward with You as a one who enjoys salvation. Help me, too, to understand that, in time, the scars of my past will fade away. Amen

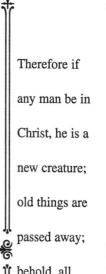

Therefore if any man be in Christ, he is a new creature; old things are passed away; behold, all things are become new.

II Corinthians 5:17 KJV

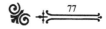

Fear with

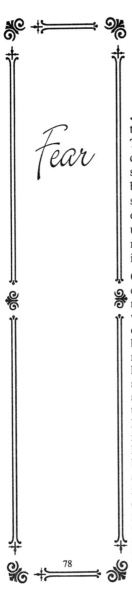

Fear

Their father had to work out-of-town leaving the mother and her children to fend for themselves. They had always known the security of having daddy there to protect them so they found themselves a bit skittish at night. Shadows appeared to be people, noises became like threats from the outside, and sleep did not come easily. Entering the dark and empty house at night was especially unnerving until the lights were turned on and the mother and young girls could see there was nothing there to harm them.

One night after returning from a late service at church, the family entered the house and the mother told the girls to hurry and get ready for bed while she went down to the basement to get a load of clothes from the dryer. Two girls went into their bedroom, still a little jittery, but ready to obey their mother. One went to the closet and as she put her hand on the door it moved back toward her every so slightly. She immediately began screaming that someone was in the closet which caused her sister to scream the same thing as the two little girls leaned against the door trying to hold the man inside. The other sister came running down the hall to see her younger sister's red faces, eyes bulged, and them shaking like leaves while putting all their force against that door while that horrible intruder just stayed in the tiny closet. The mother came rushing up from the basement, base ball bat in hand, already in tears knowing the man they were screaming about had caused great harm to them. When she looked into the bedroom and saw her daughters fighting to keep the man at bay in the

reverance.

closet she started yelling for him to come out so she could whack him with the bat. The girls quickly ran to the hall leaving their mother to fight off the foe. She took hold of the door knob and there, to her surprise was NO man ... no human at all. There was however, a tennis shoe stuck between the jam of the door and the door itself. Each time the girls pressed against the door, the tennis shoe, with its thick rubber sole, would naturally give a little, then release. The fear in that house that night was brought on by fear itself.

The Bible tells us that we are only to fear the Lord and that fear is with reverence. What is in this world can only hurt us temporarily. Are you afraid of something or someone? God is ready and able to help you conquer your fears. He can deal with the one who is hurting you and he will protect you when you cry out to Him.

Christian, let Gods distinguishing love to you motivate you to fear Him greatly. He has put His fear in your heart, and may not have given that blessing to your neighbor, perhaps not to your husband, your wife, your child, or your parent. Oh, what an obligation should this thought lay upon your heart to greatly fear the Lord! Remember also that this fear of the Lord is His treasure, a choice jewel, given only to favorites, and to those who are greatly beloved.
– John Bunyun

Father, You are big enough to protect me. Help me to be realistic about those things that are out there that will hurt me and help me to trust You in the area of fears in my life. Amen

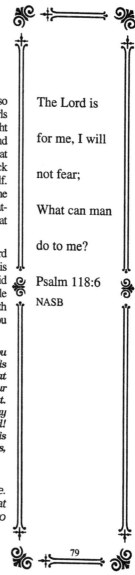

The Lord is

for me, I will

not fear;

What can man

do to me?

Psalm 118:6
NASB

Fit For Heaven's Mansion

neither death,

John Hus grew up very poor, the son of a Bohemian peasant, he was blessed to attend the University of Prague. While there he read John Wycliffe's books and was so moved by them that his life was changed and his message was very different from what he had heard all his life and from what he was preaching. It is told that he placed his hand in a fire to see if he could stand to be a martyr for Christ. He pastored the famous Bethlehem Chapel for years.

One day an order came from the Pope that all of John Wycliffe's books were to be burned. The people obeyed the order and burned them in the middle of the village square. Soon afterwards, the Pope ordered that Pastor Hus stop preaching. John Hus, with the support of his congregation took a stand against the Pope because the Pastor was only preaching the Word of God. Hus was excommunicated from the church, but he continued to preach. Finally, he was thrown into a dank and dirty dungeon cell because he refused to quit doing what God had called him to do. When told at a third hearing that if he did not stop he would die, John Hus answered, "I die gladly." In 1415 he was taken from his cell and his clothes were ripped from his body. Then he was taken outside the city and bound to a stake with straw piled all around him, a torch was lit, and the straw ignited. Pastor John

nor life, nor angels...

Hus must have recalled the fire of many years prior, but it was not until his death that for years to come Christians around the world would know that he was strong enough to be a martyr for Christ. So much like the life of Paul in Acts 5.

Literally thousands of Christians have had to lay their lives down for the cause of Christ. Most of us today can't recall the last time, if there has ever been a time, when we have had to take a stand for our beliefs. Should that occur, would you be found standing? Remember, it is most difficult to be counted in a crowd when you are sitting on the back row. Or when you have not been ground and milled for His service.

Corn, until it is pressed through the mill and is ground to powder, is not fit for bread. God so deals with us: He grinds us with grief, pain until we turn to dust, and then we are fit bread for His mansion.
– Anna Bradstreet, Puritan Poet

Lord, God, help us, I pray, to be persuaded, that neither death, nor life, nor angels, nor principalities, nor powers, nor things present, nor thing to come, nor height, nor depth, not any other creature, shall be able to separate us from the love of God, which is in Christ Jesus our Lord. Amen

And falling on his knees, he cried out with a loud voice, "Lord, do not hold this sin against them!"

Acts 7:60
NASB

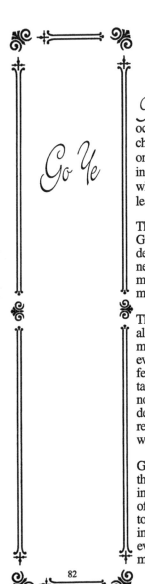

Go Ye

 here is some difference in "crossing the ocean"! Being among those with less chance to hear the truths of the Bible, makes one more of a witness. Past study and training is not vain, for situations often arise where it is necessary to use what we have learned in the most unexpected moments.

That day-by-day freshness and walk with God is the oil that lubricates the cares and demands of the day. This abiding gives needed motivation and reality to every moment, and is the Christian life lived at it's most basic.

Therefore, we must be prepared foundationally in sound doctrine and clarity of statement, so that we can anticipate questions on every issue. Even if we can think on our feet, we must have more to offer than mental concepts else, we are "of the world", and not being led by Gods Spirit. Good quality detailed preparation is essential. We need relevance (reality) and clarity (simplicity) as we minister to others.

God may place on our hearts a burden for the lost of the world and a desire to enter into the spiritual battle for men. Yet, it can often be true that witnessing and ministering to our own family and friends is intimidating and sometimes impossible. However, everything we have to give to someone on a mission field needs to be put into practice at

all nations."

home and in the local church with the body of Christ. If God can't use us here, how can He use us there?

So, no matter where God has given us our mission field, with His leading and provision, we can share the Gospel with those of any nation who have open hearts and are hungry for the knowledge of God.

We forget that the one great reason underneath all missionary enterprise is not first the elevation of the people, nor the education of the people, nor their needs; but first and foremost the command of Jesus Christ – "Go ye therefore, and teach all nations."
– Oswald Chambers

Jesus, You call each of Your children to "Go ye" although that might not mean across any ocean. It could very well mean the next room of our homes, the home across the street, the office down the hall, the county jail, the local school. Help us to accept Your call to missions and to "Go ye, therefore... and teach all..." Amen

Go ye

therefore,

and teach

all nations

Matthew 28:19
NASB

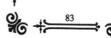

Train up

Guard

on

Guard

With evil influences jumping out at children from television these days parents need to be caution about what their children see. A young mother was teaching her three year old that television cannot be viewed without mommy being present and mommy would decide which programs were okay to watch. The little girl wanted to obey her mommy, but at three, she was confused about the good, the bad, and the ugly of television. Visiting her grandmother was a lot of fun. She was allowed to watch a safe kids show. The grandmother stepped into the kitchen for a few moments and forgot about the television being on. Suddenly, her granddaughter called to her, "Don't come in here, please," then a pause, "I'm watching something I'm not supposed to watch and I don't want you to know it!" The child, at three, was aware that she was doing something wrong, but she wanted to continue. The temptation was great yet she did not know how to hide her wrong doing. The grandmother slipped away for only a few moments and turned her attention to something else.

a child...

It only takes a second for the wrong impression to be placed before a child, who is so very impressionable. It only takes a second for us to turn our minds eyes away from our responsibility. It only takes a second to open a door for the enemy to come in like a thief in the night and devour the hearts of a child.

We need to be on guard all the time and we need to train little ones that even when those in charge fail, they must not give in to temptations. If the child's conscience convinced her, at three years old, she was doing something wrong, her conscience, at three years old, is there to help her to make a right decision.

Train up a child in the way he should go: and when he is old, he will not depart from it. – A Proverb

Jesus, sweet Jesus, help us to be aware of our responsibility to be on guard for the sneaky ways the enemy will try to rob from us and from our children. Lord, I pray that You will bring us to a place of alertness to the schemes of the devil and the ways of warfare so we can stand against the enemy. Amen

Now therefore harken unto me, O ye children: for blessed are they that keep my ways. Hear instruction, and be wise, and refuse it not.
Proverbs 8: 32, 33 KJV

a lasting

Humble Me

$\int$aint Augustine wrote for more than forty years and he ranks first place among church fathers. He wrote the Confessions of St. Augustine when he was forty-six years old. In it he confesses the sins of his youth and tells of his salvation. The book is a diary written to God praising and thanking Him for His wonderful grace in saving Augustine and calling him to serve Christ. Much like King David in the Psalms, Augustine bore his heart and soul to God.

Augustine wrote the history of man with a Christian view. His works helped to influence the Reformation of the church in the 16th century, of which the various Protestant churches came. It has been said that his work was the greatest influence in the time of the Reformation, aside from the Word of God.

impact!

Augustine is looked upon by Protestants as a forerunner of those who brought reformation to the church. His work has brought forth abundant fruit among nations and countries unheard of by the man himself.

Often what we do for Christ that makes a lasting impact on the lives of others, is never known by us. What a way to keep us humble before a holy God!

Use us, Lord, and make us humble,
Rescue us from foolish pride;
And when we begin to stumble,
Turn our thoughts to Christ who died.– Sper

God, keep me on my knees and bowed low as I do what You have commissioned me to do. Help me to be great in the kingdom, but not to know it. Amen

Humble

yourselves,

therefore,

under the

mighty hand

of God,

that He may

exalt you at the

proper time.

I Peter 5:6
NASB

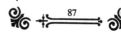

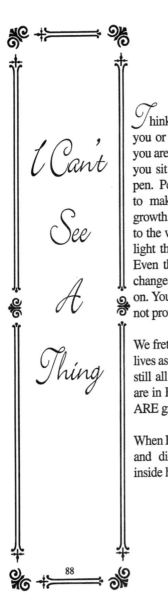

I Can't See A Thing

$\mathscr{T}$hink for a moment, about a potted plant you or someone else owns. Now, say that you are going to watch that plant grow. As you sit and watch, nothing seems to happen. Perhaps you should measure the plant to make certain you aren't missing the growth. You water the plant and you take it to the window to give it plenty of the sunlight that it needs. Still, you see nothing. Even though you don't and can't see any change, there is growth and change going on. You know that, but your naked eye cannot prove it.

We fret about not seeing any growth in our lives as Christians. We try 'this and that' and still all appears as before. God says if we are in His will (by surrender and faith) we ARE growing.

When Elisha saw the seed fall in the ground and die something was still growing – inside him – and it was faith!

path may fade...

So often we are so harsh on ourselves that we actually interrupt the growth process. God is always at work in the lives of Christians.

The Lord wants us to walk by faith, because our eyes can be deceived: And even though our path may fade, Gods Word can always be believed.
– Anon

I pray, O Lord, that I will not trust my senses when it comes to spiritual matters, but trust the living and reliable Word of God in faith to see Your timeless truths. Amen

... we walk by faith, not sight

II Corinthians 5:7 NASB

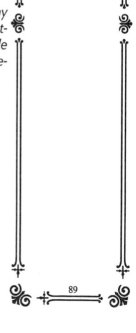

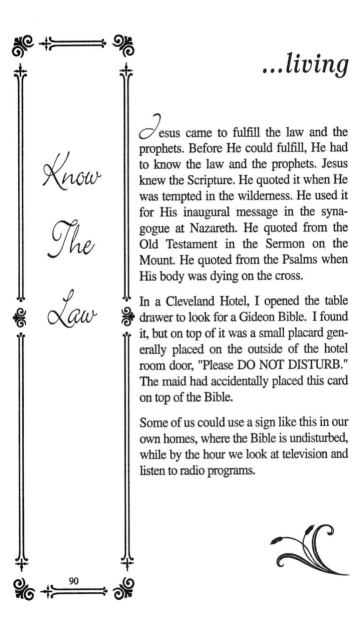

...living

Know The Law

Jesus came to fulfill the law and the prophets. Before He could fulfill, He had to know the law and the prophets. Jesus knew the Scripture. He quoted it when He was tempted in the wilderness. He used it for His inaugural message in the synagogue at Nazareth. He quoted from the Old Testament in the Sermon on the Mount. He quoted from the Psalms when His body was dying on the cross.

In a Cleveland Hotel, I opened the table drawer to look for a Gideon Bible. I found it, but on top of it was a small placard generally placed on the outside of the hotel room door, "Please DO NOT DISTURB." The maid had accidentally placed this card on top of the Bible.

Some of us could use a sign like this in our own homes, where the Bible is undisturbed, while by the hour we look at television and listen to radio programs.

and powerful!

We do not disturb the Bible because the daily reading of Gods Word will disturb us. "Love your neighbor as yourself" is disturbing. "Seek ye first the kingdom of God, and His righteousness" does not tend to lull us to complacent living.

Jesus knew the law and Jesus fulfilled it. We must know the law if we are to fulfill it. – Copied

The word of God is living and powerful. St. Paul

Help me, Father to know Your Word so I can be a living example of Your law. Amen

Do not think

that I came

to abolish the

Law or the

prophets;

I did not come

to abolish, but

to fulfill.

Matthew 5:17
NASB

Life

Changing

Experience

the road

*E*ven as that day on the road to Damascus was the turning point in Paul's life, so it was also the turning point in the history of the apostolic churches. God revealed to Paul the need of the Gentile world. His chief mission was to the Gentiles, but he did not exclude the Jews. As he went from town to town, preaching the message of salvation, he first entered the Jewish synagogue and preached to them as long as they would listen. But when they did not listen, he turned to the Gentiles, who were hungry for the Words of Life.

Paul obeyed the Great Commission of our Lord, "Go ye therefore, and teach all nations, baptizing them in the name of the Father, and the Son, and of the Holy Ghost." He spent his life carrying the Gospel to nations round about him.

It was at Antioch, a Gentile church, where believers were first called Christians. It was also at Antioch where Paul began his active public ministry among the Gentiles. This church sent forth the first missionaries, Paul and Barnabas. During his public ministry,

to Damascus

which covered a quarter of a century. Paul completed three great missionary journeys, made five visits to Jerusalem, and spent at least four years prison in Caesarea and Rome.

Paul labored more than all the other apostles, but yet he considered himself "the least of the apostles." – Borrowed

No condemnation now I dread,
I am my Lord's and He is mine;
Alive in Him, my living Head,
And clothed in righteousness divine.
-- Charles Wesley

God, what an evil man Paul was before he met You and before You transformed him on the road to Damascus. You will be doing the same in the lives of lost souls until You return for Your bride. Help us to remember our conversion and be as enthusiastic about "winning the lost at any cost" now as we were then. Amen

And it came about that as he journeyed, he was approaching Damascus, and suddenly a light from heaven flashed around him ...

he is a chosen instrument of Mine, to bear My name before the Gentiles and kings and the sons of Israel...

Acts 9:1, 15
NASB

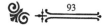

Rahab, Used by God

He forgets

She was probably one of the most wicked women in all Jerico. In any city she would have been considered very wicked. She was probably one of the lowest women on morality of her time.

She was, however, transformed, by God. Then she risked her own life to save two of Gods servants, and cooperated in every way to fulfill Gods purposes. She and her house were spared from sure destruction because of her actions.

Most of us have felt that God would never forgive something we did and He would never be able to use us for good. God takes lives, no matter where they have been, and transforms them. Then, He uses them for good.

the past.

Our God is a God of the future, not the past. He forgives so completely that He forgets the past. The past will be overshadowed by a more glorious future in Him.
– Dr. V. Gilbert Beers, *The Book of Life*

God, we all have a past, some pretty awful. You are a God of futures and I pray You will transform us out of the pit and into Your glorious light. Amen

By faith,

Rahab the

Harlot, did not

perish ...

Hebrews 11:31
NASB

Super

Hero

Samson

supernatural

Kids today are excited and energized by all the Super Hero figures in the market place. It might surprise them to learn that there are many real life Super Heroes in the Bible. Samson, a Great Super Hero, was able to defeat whole armies and was feared by all because of his might. Supernaturally, Samson did more physically than all of the naturally strong men in that day. The Lord was truly his strength, and He knew it. Just like in the life of Samson, our strength leaves us at the first sign of sin. Sin hinders Gods power in our lives, and we, too, can be bound by Satan as a prisoner. Power and strength come from separation unto the Lord, not separation from the world. Separation from the world without separation unto God leaves a dry, dead life.

When Samson turned from God, he lost everything he had. All left him, but the Lord accepted him when he came back in repentance. When Samson returned he looked normal physically, and his source

power

of strength could not be determined; those around him had to ask him where he got his strength.

He had a secret! The Lord was his strength. The Spirit gave him supernatural power and we can show children for generations to come that with Christ they become powerful in the kingdom of God here on earth.

Even though we may not look or appear to be anything or anyone special, God can do with us whatever He likes. He is not hindered if we belong fully to Him.

The worlds Super Heroes receive their strength from fantasy; Gods Super Heroes receive their strength from the rock, Jesus Christ.
– DC Hummel

Father, our strength comes from You. I pray we will come to the well often to draw from it. Amen

> The Lord
>
> is my strength
>
> and my shield...
>
> Psalm 28:7
> NASB

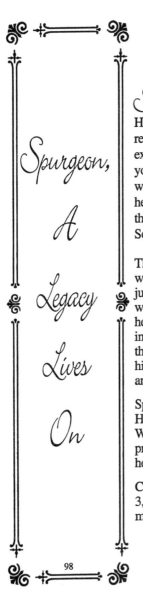

Spurgeon, A Legacy Lives On

backed by

Spurgeon was an eager student of God. He learned quickly, but had many times of review and added study in the faith. He experienced the fight of faith from his youth up. The most tender part of his life was a message he dictated to friends before he passed into glory. His final words were those of faith in God. He lived and died in Sovereign hands.

This workman was far above others, yet he was not conscious of it. As a person he was just good-natured. His sermon illustrations were clear and from everyday events. He helped everyone that he could, as is shown in his orphanages, his home for the elderly, the ministerial school he founded, and in his practical care for pastors through literary and monetary means.

Spurgeon could not live apart from prayer. His life long devotion and study to the Word of God was backed up by earnest prayer. He fully believed in prayer because he fully believed in God.

C. H. Spurgeon died in 1892, but more than 3,000 of his sermons exist in print today for millions to read and learn from.

earnest prayer

Spurgeon knew that it took work to be successful in the Kingdom, labor that was more difficult in the years he lived in England, but he also knew the way to accomplish that work was by first getting down on his knees. He left a legacy for all Christians in his writings and sermons, but the greatest legacy was of the man who was devoted to Jesus Christ.

My brethren, let me say, be like Christ at all times. Imitate Him in "public." Most of us live in some sort of public capacity – many of us are called to work before our fellow men, every day. We are watched; our words are caught; our lives are examined – taken to pieces. The eagle-eyed, argus-eyed world observes everything we do, and sharp critics are upon us. Let us live the life of Christ in public. Let us take care that we exhibit our Master, and not ourselves – so that we can say, "It is no longer I that live, but Christ that lives in me." – Charles H. Spurgeon

Father, help us to be sensitive to the ways we portray You before the world. Amen

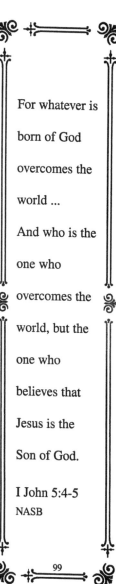

For whatever is born of God overcomes the world ...
And who is the one who overcomes the world, but the one who believes that Jesus is the Son of God.

I John 5:4-5
NASB

Teach Me Thy Way, O Lord...

Gods Will For

$\mathcal{C}$hrist has the credentials to teach us anything He wants us to know! He's Board Certified!

We are capable of learning anything He wants us to know. He knows truth because He is truth. He teaches all day, every day, and He teaches for life! His class room is the world. His tests are our trials and tribulations and He promised we would have them! Pop Quiz's come on a regular basis and can be short and take only a few minutes or they can last a long time! The topic is always the same... Gods Will For Your Life 101! A prerequisite for a good teacher is that they know their students. Well, He knew us while we were still in our mothers womb. He knows the hairs on our head... each of our heads. He speaks our native tongue... nationality and location are not barriers for Him. He knows the content of each lesson, He knows each pupil by name, and He knows the means to teach what He wants to teach.

Your Life 101

Our responsibility should then be to sit back and get ready for the greatest lesson of all. "Teach me Thy ways, O Lord."

Teaching, promotes learning, learning is fueled by faith.
Faith comes by hearing, and hearing by the word of God.
– DC Hummel

Dear Jesus, I want to sit at Your feet and learn all You want to teach me. Help me, I pray, to be a pupil that will learn quickly and one that will apply Your timeless truths to my life daily.
Amen

My son, give

attention to

My words ...

for they are

life to those

who

find them.

Proverbs
4:20-22
NASB

Train up

Thanks-giving

$\mathcal{I}$n December 1621, the people of Plymouth Colony celebrated "in gratitude for the ending of a difficult year and for a successful harvest." This became our model for Thanksgiving.

Thanksgiving Day in America is rooted in routine tradition, the idea of a day set apart to celebrate the completion of the harvest and to render homage to the Spirit who caused the fruits and crops to grow is ancient and universal.

As children of God we are to be in an attitude of prayer and thanksgiving every day for we are a blessed people. God is our Savior and Lord, He is our Shepherd, our teacher, our healer, our provider, our protector, our everything. His bounty is before us and around us all the time.

a child...

As we partake of Thanksgiving dinner, or any dinner for that matter, let's recall the sacrifices made to bring a variety of seeds and ideas for planting and harvesting to our nation and to our tables. We have so much to be thankful for, don't we?

Come, ye thankful people, come,
Raise the song of harvest home:
All is safely gathered in,
Ere the winter storms begin;
God, our Maker, doth provide
For our wants to be supplied;
Come to God's own temple, come,
Raise the song of harvest home.
– George J. Elvey

Lord of the harvest, thank You for every thing You give to us. You provide for us in ways that are so amazing. We are grateful for the harvest, but grateful, too, for the dry seasons for they help us to trust You. Amen

Blessed be the Lord, who daily loadeth us with benefits...

Psalm 68:19
KJV

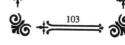

Where is your

The King of Kings

 ritish minister James Ussher from the 17th century is best known for his chronology of Biblical events. While preaching before a Covent Garden congregation the church doors flew open and an ornately attired messenger, with an official looking paper, entered and moved to the front of the church. Ussher immediately came down from the pulpit and asked, "What is the reason for this interruption?"

"I, sir, am here at the behest of His Majesty with a communication for James Ussher." "I am he, " answered the minister.

"You are hereby directed to come at once to London and appear before the king. His Majesty urgently requests your immediate visit."

Ussher looked out at the congregation of Englishman hungry for the Word of God. Then he looked at the king's orders. Should he just up and leave without delivering his sermon?

After a moment's hesitation he made a decision. "Sir, at the moment I am engaged in the business of the King of kings and I must first discharge my obligation to Him, but as

allegiance?

soon as I have finished here, I will hasten to London to learn the pleasure of the King of England!"

Then he went back to the pulpit and delivered his message!

Where is your allegiance? There may be times when rushing to the call of a leader is exactly what we are supposed to do. After all, it was Christ who said we are to honor our leaders. There are, though, priorities that we need to have in place in our lives so we will know when to rush and when to stay and complete the work at hand.

Majestic sweetness sits enthroned Upon the Savior's brow; His head with radiant glories crowed, His lips with grace o'erflow. No mortal can with Him compare, Among the sons of men; Fairer is He than all the fair, That fill the heavenly train.
– Hugh Wilson

Father, I pray that my priorities will be in order and that I will know to whom my allegiance belongs. Thank You for timeless truths we learn from great saints of old. Amen

He who is

the blessed

and only

Sovereign, the

King of kings

and

Lord of lords...

I Timothy 6:15
NASB

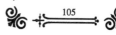

Treasure Awaits

A former pastor stressed the importance of reading scripture each time as if it is the first. Forgetting what we know and allowing God to speak through His Word what He wants us to glean from its pages. Reading the Bible is like a new treasure hunt every day. Morsels that seemed unavailable before are now clearly there for the gathering.

The times we live in require something that we can embrace. The Bible offers what we need to live in these times of uncertainty and turmoil. So many are grasping for whatever the newest fad is and they find, after a while, that they have nothing substantial to rely on.

Treasures await the one who takes the Word of God in hand and carefully moves from page to page looking for nuggets for life. A few moments each day can make a world of difference in a life that has no hope or direction.

every day

Not knowing when the dawn will come I open every door.
– *Emily Dickinson*

Dear Lord, Your Word is a gift to Your children filled with wonderful treasures that never run out. Thank You for blessing us with more than we can ever grasp here on earth, but for what we will enjoy in abundance in heaven.
Amen

For the word of

God is living

and active...

Hebrews 4:12
NASB

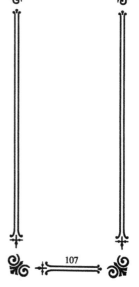

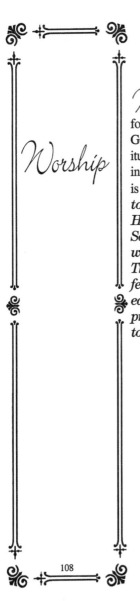

The reason we

*W*orship is the highest expression of that for which we are created. In true Worship God is all that matters. True worship is spiritual – we are in the Spirit. The Holy Spirit in us is to be the life of the glorified Jesus as is expressed in Psalm 66... *Shout joyfully to God, all the earth; Sing the glory of His name; Make His praise glorious. Say to God, "How awesome are Thy works! Because of the greatness of Thy power Thine enemies will give feigned obedience to Thee. All the earth will worship Thee And will sing praises to Thee, They will sing praises to Thy name."*

exist is.....

The reason we exist is not just to have big, happy churches. We are to live and worship and proclaim the Word of God to the nations and peoples of the earth. This will drive back the powers of darkness and implement every intention of the heart of God. -- Dean Sherman

God, in heaven, I worship You, I adore You, I honor You. Amen

Worship

the Lord with

reverence...

Psalm 2:11
NASB

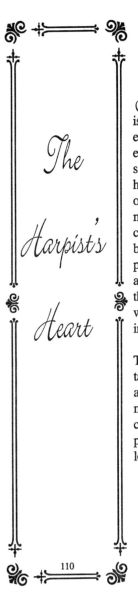

The Harpist's Heart

sweet communion

She could not get the money in the register to balance no matter how many different times she counted it. Three other employees had tried to come up with the same total, but all to no avail. It was an hour past time to leave the store so everyone left except the manager and one staff member. That staff member went to her car and came back with her harp. She sat behind the manager and after she had prayed, she began to play and sing. It was as if the heavens angels filled that store as the most wonderful calm came over the whole place and without even understanding how, the receipts balanced.

The Harpist and the manager have often talked about that night... that night when angelic music was the basis for sweet communion with Christ. That night when the calmness was necessary in order to complete the arduous task before them. The fellowship was amazing, wondrous, and alive.

with Christ

Christ wants us to experience sweet times of fellowship with Him... even when everything around us appears to be nothing but gloom. Just take a moment and listen, listen to the angels as they play soft music to console you while you work.

Praise You, God, for precious friends who take extra time to minister to us. God bless my friend, the Harpist. May her times playing bring comfort to those who need it and may her music forever bless You. Amen

I will also

praise Thee

with a harp,

Even Thy truth,

O my God...

Psalm 71:22

NASB

Caring Counselor

$\mathcal{I}$ know a Christian counselor who has such a poor memory that he feels he is in the perfect field. Once he counsels a person he completely forgets what they have said. So, for him, a confidence is genuinely a confidence. He always has to refer to his notes in order to remember the details of what his clients are going through. Now, that's the counselor most of us would love to have. He can certainly be trusted to not reveal confidential information about us.

God is our counselor, too, and He already knows about our deepest and darkest secrets and sins. We can tell Him anything and He will always listen. He never tries to tear us down or destroy us. He goes beyond what most counselors are able to do and He loves us.

What more can a person ask for in a counselor. Well, He not only counsels, He helps us to reach our potential, He makes a way for us, He provides the means, He has

my soul......

given us a manuel to follow. All we have to do is to go to Him for consultation. His office never closes and He never uses an answering machine. He is available to us. As has been so aptly stated, "He is just a prayer away."

Be still, my soul; thy God doth undertake,
To guide the future as He has the past.
Thy Hope, thy confidence a thing to shake;
All now mysterious shall be bright at last.
Be still, my soul; the waves and winds still know
His voice who ruled them while He dwelt below.

Lord Jesus, help us, we pray, to run to You and to acknowledge You as counselor. Amen

Casting all your care upon Him; for he careth for you.

I Peter 5:7 KJV

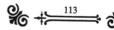

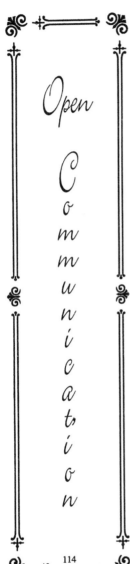

Open Communication

He wants to hear

*W*e hear so much today about Open Communication. To some the term means we have the right to say whatever we want, whenever we please. To the television industry that seems to mean people should be allowed to discuss even those things that are done in secret, which the Bible says is wrong. We are not to talk about things people do in the dark. However, we Christians do need to communicate with Christ. Communication with Christ means to talk and to listen.

David talked with God in a way many Christians today aren't able to. He did so because he knew God, as Lord and Savior, yes, but also as friend. There was a level of trust that is foundational in any relationship when such freedom can be expressed. David cried out to God about his most intimate feelings and desires. He knew God welcomed him as a son. He understood the unconditional love God had for him. Open and honest communication does not just allow for the great, and even, the good stuff about us to spring forth. When based on a solid commitment to a person and to that relationship, communication allows for freedom to talk about every aspect of life – good,

about everything...

detail that is important to the person. When was the last time you talked with God? Really talked and then really listened to hear what He has to say? If we can trust Him with our praises, why can't we trust Him with our problems? He wants to hear about everything that is a part of our lives.

It is not the bee's touching of the flower that gathers honey, but her abiding for a time upon the flower that draws out the sweet. It's not he that reads most, but he that mediates most, that will prove the choicest, sweetest, wisest and strongest Christian. – Thomas Brooks

Father, God, help me to love You so much that I will trust You with all of me, everything about me. Please help me to be willing to climb up on Your lap and spend time talking with You and listening to You. Lord, God, Jehovah, help me to tell You all about my life and to be willing to lay the bad reports at the foot of the cross, but to shout out freely the praises on my lips to You, O Holy God. Amen

Out of the depths I have cried to Thee, Lord. Lord hear my voice!

Psalm 130:1
NASB

comfort

Praise

You,

O God!

$\mathcal{T}$he Psalmist, David, vowed to praise God. His deep and committed love for God is evident throughout the book of Palms. The relationship he had with God allowed him freedom to express, in song, praises that bring comfort to our hearts and music to our voices even today. David was able to express all of his feelings, whether good or bad. He took liberty as he shouted his praises. Summarily, he did not refrain from expressing displeasure with his circumstances. He cried out to God about everything. He was open and honest. He was not afraid to speak out against those who fought against him. He willingly asked God to *"rise up...draw also the spear and the battle ax to meet those who pursue me. Let those be ashamed and dishonored who seek my life." Psalm 35*

to our hearts

God knows all, but He wants us, His children, to shout out our joys and praise Him. He also welcomes our tears and daily concerns. He never tires of hearing from his children.

Praise, my soul, the King of heaven, To His feet thy tribute bring; Ransomed, healed, restored, forgiven, Who, like me His praise should sing? Alleluia! Alleluia! Praise the Everlasting King!

O Lord, I call upon Thee; Hasten to me! Give ear to my voice when I call to Thee! May my prayer be counted as incense before Thee ... Amen

My heart is steadfast, O God; I will sing, I will sing praises, even with my soul, Awake, harp and Lyre; I will awaken the dawn! I will give thanks to Thee, O Lord, among the peoples; And I will sing praises to Thee among the nations.

Psalm 108: 1 - 3
NASB

For His

*H*er husband drove around the block for the third time trying to find a parking space on the crowed city street, on a blustery winters' day. As she glanced back and forth from one side of the street to the other hoping to help locate an empty space, she noticed a tattered elderly woman. The old woman wasn't wearing a coat, gloves, or hat even though the temperatures were well below freezing. She could barely shuffle her feet as the harsh wind pushed her frail body in the opposite direction. The thought passed the mind of the young woman in the car that perhaps she should offer her coat to the old lady. At that moment her husband turned the car at the next street corner. When they came back to the main street the elderly fragile woman was nowhere in sight.

Was this a missed opportunity to be a blessing to someone in obvious need? We don't know what might have been. However, Christians should be so aware of the prompting of the Holy Spirit in us that we will know when to reach out and when to sit still.

In order to know His will we must first have a relationship with Father God. The Bible tells us to abide in Christ and let Him abide in us, and that requires Bible study and prayer.

Names Sake

He promises to give us His wisdom, knowledge, and understanding to discern how and when to reach out, and to whom. He will also tell us when to not take any action other than to pray. When the Lord is working in the life of one in need He may have to allow that person to struggle without the assistance of well meaning Christian friends as was the case of the Prodigal son. Our help could actually be a hindrance to what the Lord is doing.

The memory of that day driving around looking for a parking space has caused the young woman to consider her own motives for giving and the lessons from that day have been life changing ones. She is content and peaceful now when He tells her to give and when He says to not do anything... short of praying.

God wants us to be cheerful givers. He also wants us to give according to His purposes, laying down our own feelings, for His Names Sake. Period!

Father God, I need Your wisdom to know when to give, how to give, and the way to present my gift. Help me to not consider self when giving, but to give as unto You. Help me, too, Lord Jesus, to love You so much that I will give You the time you need to make me the sweet aroma of Christ. Amen

And the people asked Him, saying, What shall we do then? He answereth and saith unto them, He that hath two coats, let him impart to him that hath none; and he that hath meat, let him do likewise.

Luke 3:10,11
KJV

No Good Thing Will He Withhold

...purple

The thirteen year old was beginning to feel the pressures of being a teenager. Pier pressure was a constant companion and her mother realized her daughter was struggling. After a week of the most outrageous behavior the mother had no choice but to pull the reins and restrict her daughter. There were many lessons to be learned over the next few weeks as mother and daughter talked through the issue of anger and greed. The mother explained that God wanted to give her His best and it was up to her to not look for anything less. After some time of counsel she was willing to move back over to where she needed to be under her mothers authority. It was a wonderful thing to see this young girl, so confused by her life and the world around her, come to the foot of the cross and ask God to forgive her.

Some time later, when a very special Youth trip came up the mother agreed that her daughter could go. The fee for the trip was all the mother could afford but her daughter would have to carry an old, really old, piece of luggage. The daughter said if she could have a new purple suit case she would be the happiest person in the world. The girl did not beg, she simply made the statement. However, the mother heard and recalled the lessons her daughter had just learned. So, she prayed that God would help her to bless her daughter with His best and let her have a purple suit case. The mother, who had never even seen purple luggage, prayed that if there

leather luggage

was one piece of purple luggage in the whole city that God would lead her to it and that the price would be within her meager budget.

A few days passed when the mother stopped at a local mall and upon entry into a store she found herself facing the biggest pile of luggage she had ever seen assembled in one place and in every size and color imaginable. At the very top of the pile was the most beautiful, perfectly sized for a thirteen year old, piece of purple leather luggage! When the sales clerk finally got it from the pile she said, "We just threw it up there for color, not thinking anyone would ever want it." The price was an amazing $10! The mother left the store that day in tears and rushed home to surprise her daughter.

When her daughter arrived home from school she went into her room and on her bed was probably the only piece of purple luggage in the whole state ... it was Gods "good thing" for his little daughter who was learning how to trust her Father God.

God, in His wisdom, knows what "good things" we need and when to give them to us. The timeless truth is that He will not withhold good things, because He promised not to.

Abba, Father, You have so many "good things" You want to give to Your children. Help us to walk uprightly so we can receive Your gifts for Your Names Sake. Amen

Better is a little with the fear of the Lord, Than great treasure with trouble.

Proverbs 15:16

NKJV

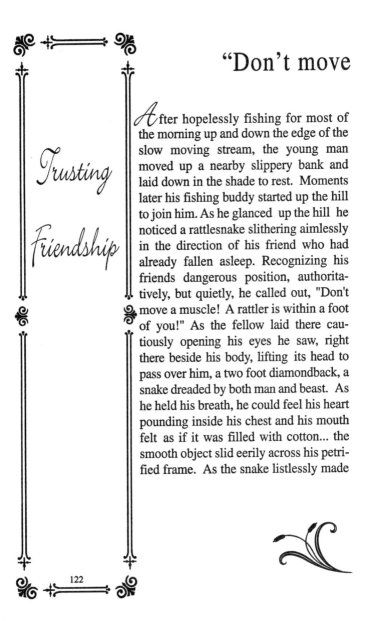

"Don't move

Trusting

Friendship

After hopelessly fishing for most of the morning up and down the edge of the slow moving stream, the young man moved up a nearby slippery bank and laid down in the shade to rest. Moments later his fishing buddy started up the hill to join him. As he glanced up the hill he noticed a rattlesnake slithering aimlessly in the direction of his friend who had already fallen asleep. Recognizing his friends dangerous position, authoritatively, but quietly, he called out, "Don't move a muscle! A rattler is within a foot of you!" As the fellow laid there cautiously opening his eyes he saw, right there beside his body, lifting its head to pass over him, a two foot diamondback, a snake dreaded by both man and beast. As he held his breath, he could feel his heart pounding inside his chest and his mouth felt as if it was filled with cotton... the smooth object slid eerily across his petrified frame. As the snake listlessly made

a muscle!"

When God allows us to experience a thing, it is for our benefit, but for the benefit of those around us. These two young men were friends. There was a level of trust between them. When one told the other to not move, he did not. Once the snake had moved on out of the way, the one in authority at the time did not boast, rather, he praised the calmness of his friend. The one who had been spared, and who was obviously shaken, showed gratitude to his friend for giving the order that saved his life. They were there for one another, but there was a relationship in place before the incident that gave creedance to the order given and the reception of that order. Then, in the end, they were both blessed, and now, so are we!

Lord, thank You for every situation You allow us to go through for us and for those around us. Thank You that we can trust You to help us to build quality relationships that include trust and respect. Relationships that mean we put another's needs before our own. Amen

...there is a

friend that sticks

closer than a

brother.

Proverbs 18:24
NASB

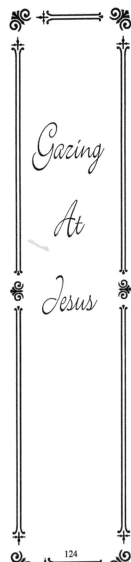

Gazing

At

Jesus

In church recently I noticed Sam was holding his daughter, Jaalanne, who is less than two years old. As he was singing and listening to the message she gazed up at his face. Completely oblivious to what was going on around her, she starred up at her daddy with deep admiration. Suddenly, Jaalanne reached up and kissed him on his cheek. That kiss was followed by a couple dozen more. She smiled as she hugged his neck and kissed him from one side of his face to the other. She gazed into his eyes and looked at him admiringly and kissed him some more. She was clueless to the people around her, to the voices singing, to any words spoken... her heart and mind were fixed on her father. She loved him and adored him, and honored him right there in church. His wife looked over at their daughter loving on her daddy and smiled as if to reinforce the love between them. After a few moments Sam had to lay his child back in his arms, but she never took her eyes off of his face.

What a beautiful picture of how Christ wants us to gaze upon His face and love on Him. He wants us to be unaware, as if dead, of the concerns around us and fix our eyes on Him.

on her father.

Perhaps you have not experienced that kind of deep emotional love for anyone since your wedding day or since you bore a child. Perhaps you have never experienced a love that is so deep you lose sight of the cares around you. Christ Jesus wants us to know that kind of depth in our relationship to him. It's okay to love on Him today with eyes fixed upon His face oblivious to what is around you... just seeking His face and loving Him.

Lord Jesus Christ, we seek Thy face; Within the veil we bow the knee, Oh, let Thy glory fill the place, And bless us while we wait on Thee. The brow that once with thorns was bound, Thy hands, Thy side, we fain would see, Draw near, Lord Jesus, glory-crowned, And bless us while we wait on Thee.

Jesus, I want to gaze upon Your face the same way a little child does their earthly father, oblivious to what is around me, just fixing my eyes upon You. Amen

And look upon

the face of

Thine anointed.

Psalm 84:9
NASB

Looking

Upward

The story goes that the sea looked toward heaven gazing upon the beauty of the puffy white clouds and wanted to be a cloud. The sea worked very hard until it tossed itself up in the air only to fall back upon a rock. No use, the sea could not be a cloud. The sun watching the struggle below said to the sea, "Be quiet, be still, and just look at me." The sea obeyed and was quiet and stopped struggling. The sun began to shine brighter and brighter and the sea felt its moisture moving upward until suddenly, next to the puffy white cloud appeared a second cloud. What the sea could not do no matter how hard he tried, the sun was able to do simply because the sea looked to it.

We, too, struggle in our Christian life to do everything we can to become like Christ, often to no avail. All God wants us to do is to look to Him, and He will transform us into His likeness.

look at me.

Days there may be of joy, and deep delight, when earth seems fairest, and her skies most bright;
Then draw me closer to Thee, lest I rest, elsewhere, my Savior, than upon Thy breast.

I Take Thy Promise, Lord
– F. C. Goudimel

Lord, God, how assuring to know that in Your great creativity, You made all things come together in perfect beauty and splendor. Thank You. Amen

The Lord will

accomplish

what concerns

me; Thy

lovingkindness,

O Lord,

is everlasting,

Psalm 138:8
NASB

acquainted

No Needs

$\mathcal{O}$nce we know Christ as Lord and Savior, understanding that He is our Shepherd and knowing the attributes of a Shepherd will enhance our walk with Him. A Shepherd meets all the needs of the sheep he tends. Sheep learn very early to recognize the voice, smell, and movements of their Shepherd. Sheep will not easily go with a different Shepherd. They fear the intruder and shy away.

The Lord is the Shepherd of born again believers. He promised to be, so there is no question about His position. We get to know His voice as we meditate on His word and listen to Him in times of prayer.

As our Shepherd He provides for us --- everything! We are so often concerned about food and housing that we overlook all the ways the Lord does provide. Psalm 23:1b says, "I shall not want..." which implies, I shall not want for anything -- materially, physically, emotionally, or spiritually. Our Shepherd does provide food and housing, but He leads

with our grief

us to the right school, job, mate, church, and in all areas of our life.

Everything we need in every area is available through Him. He is our counselor, High Priest, provider, purse barer. He hears out cries, He is acquainted with our grief, He shelters us.

I would appear that with all our needs met we would stop complaining and moaning and simply trust Him. He knows how difficult it is for us to just trust.

There is no other who can be Christ.

Father, God, thank You for being my all. I pray that I will literally fall into Your arms allowing You to have complete control of me and all that concerns me. Amen

I shall

not want ...

Psalm 23:1
NASB

Saints In The Making

acquainted

God did not promise us an easy life once we get saved. Actually, He tells us that we will have trials and tribulations. Some seem to walk through their trials unscathed while others struggle to understand and/or accept that Christ is the one who is in control. It is important to understand that culture, background, life style, all play a role in the way we react to trials.

Some cry and scream, others get angry, some retreat into their own world, while many talk excessively about their problems. We are all uniquely and wonderfully made so it can be expected that we will react to circumstances in our lives in uniquely different ways.

My times are in Thy hand; My God, I wish them there; My life, my friends, my soul I leave Entirely to Thy care. My times are in Thy hands: Why should I doubt or fear? My Father's hand will never cause His child a needless tear. – William F. Lloyd

in Thy hand...

When God makes a saint, He uses the sharpest knives on His turning lathe as well. he cannot shape one without pain, but He never uses needless pain. All is chosen in relationship to one's eternal vocation.
– *Paul E. Billheimer*

Dear Jesus, thank You for the way You made me. Help me to, Lord, to make room for You to continue working in my life so I will react to trials and pain knowing that it is not needless when You are in it. Amen

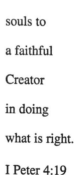

Therefore, let those also who suffer according to the will of God entrust their souls to a faithful Creator in doing what is right.

I Peter 4:19
NASB

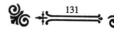

He died...

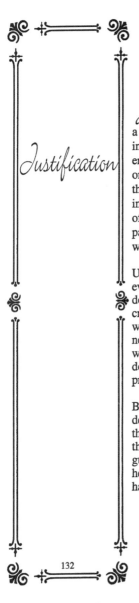

Justification

$\mathcal{A}$ famous Frenchman was once tried for a crime and found guilty. He protested his innocence to the last, but was sentenced, nevertheless, and condemned to lifelong imprisonment. Some time later it was discovered that a mistake had been made and that he was innocent after all. Immediately the president of the republic pardoned him, and quickly the pardon was taken to the prison in which he was confined.

Upon the presentation, to the amazement of everyone, he refused it. "I don't want a pardon," he exclaimed. "I am not guilty of any crime. How can the president pardon me when I am already innocent? I will have a new trial and be declared innocent, or else I will remain where I am. Away with your pardon. I don't want it." And there the adamant prisoner stayed.

Before long his friends got busy. They demanded a rehearing of his case. At last they were successful. He was tried again, and the verdict rendered this time was "not guilty." He walked out of the court with his head held up, and faced the world a free man, having been justified by the courts of France.

in your stead...

That is what God can do for you. Not because you are innocent, for "all have sinned" and are guilty, but because Jesus Christ bore the penalty of your guilt in His body on the Cross.

He died in your stead, took your place, and now, since your sin, all of it, has been imputed to Him, God can justify you, and account you righteous. He can pronounce you "not guilty." Justification is the judicial act of God whereby He declares righteous one who believes in Christ. – Borrowed

See that justice is done, let mercy be your first concern, and humbly obey your God. The Prophet Micah

Lord. God, I pray that we will seek justice, Your justice in our courts today. That never an innocent one is placed behind bars for a crime he did not commit. We pray for Your wisdom. Amen

God is the

one who

justifies...

Romans 8:33
NASB

Stand

Firm

Christian experience begins with sitting and leads to walking, but it does not end with these. Every Christian must also learn to STAND!
– Manley Beasley

It takes stamina to stand so the body must be prepared to stand for long periods of time. Sir Frances Drake said, "Permanence, perseverance, and persistence in spite of all obstacles, discouragements, and impossibilities: It is this, that in all things distinguishes the strong soul from the weak."

Timeless truths come from Gods Word that will give us the strength we need to move forward for Christ while we labor in the Kingdom of God, here on earth.

truths

Father, blessings upon You for Your timeless truths that are available to us every moment of everyday. We love You, Lord. Amen

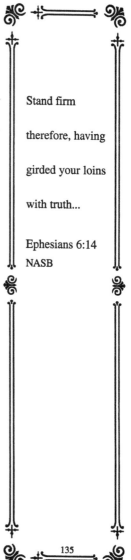

Stand firm

therefore, having

girded your loins

with truth...

Ephesians 6:14
NASB

The Needy Delivered

It is the needy whom God hears in prayer. To approach the throne of an eastern king with a petition, one must needs bear costly gifts to win his favor. But ours is a God of grace. "Like as a father pitieth his children, so the Lord pitieth them that fear Him." He asks no gift of colored gems. But bending down to us in infinite love He says; "My child how needy are you? What heavy burden is upon you? What grievous sorrow is darkening your faith? What fear of future ill is shadowing your pathway? What spiritual thirst do you want slaked? What barrenness of soul enriched? How hungry, how helpless, how faint, how hopeless are you?

What do you need this hour? For I will deliver the needy." And so the very need that burdens, dispirits and perplexes us is at once the condition and pledge of His blessing. God's clouds pour refreshing showers upon the sun-parched fields because of their need. God's sun quickens the seed, feeds the plant, and paints the flower because of need. "He shall deliver the needy ... and him that hath no helper." Have you reached a crisis in life where the gloom is so dense, the guidance so uncertain, the burden so heavy, that you have come to the end of all your own resources?

a miracle.

You have studied and planned, striven and sought, until baffled at every turn you sink in utter defeat and moan, "There is no help for me; I must give up the fight." Then understand that you are just the man God is looking for -- just the one who is ripe for deliverance -- just the special individual to whom His promise is made. "For He shall deliver the needy ... and him that hath no helper." Do not be too afraid of getting into the spot where you have no helper, for that is the spot where, like Jacob, you will meet a delivering God. Do not be too anxious to be free from needs, unless you want to be free from prayer power. Accept them just as God sends them or permits them. The moment you come to a need, remember also that you have come to a promise. "He shall deliver the needy." To miss a need may be to miss a miracle. As soon as one appears in your life, do not begin to worry because it is there, but praise God because it is to be supplied. -- Borrowed

Father, Your heart is full of compassion toward the poor and the needy. We are all needy. Help us to draw from You all we need. Amen

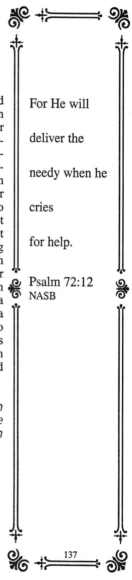

For He will deliver the needy when he cries for help.

Psalm 72:12
NASB

And to

Bring Ye All The Tithes

The college student stood before the congregation explaining that he had never tithed. He simply did not feel he could. It was all he could do to manage his bills while and student and have a little money left to purchase food. "Besides, God really didn't need his money. It's not like God is poor or anything. Doesn't the Bible say that God owns the cattle on a thousand hills?" Something was happening in this fellows heart because the question of tithing kept coming up.

In church the next week the pastor preached on ... you guessed it ... tithing. The pastor made it clear that God does not need money. There went that objection. And the pastor explained that bringing the tithes to the storehouse (the church) did not mean more money for the pastor. He went on to tell how the tithe is used ... to support missionaries, whose pictures and information were posted on the Missions Board, and to care for the building where services were held. He also explained the churches emergency fund for displaced families, medical needs of church members, and to meet the needs of those who have suffered loss. The pastor went down the list abolishing all the negatives and preconceived ideas the young man had about the

top it all off...

way the tithe is used (misused) and why he should have no part in such. The minister went on to explain that God blesses those who give, that no one can out give God. The student was so convicted and convinced that he should tithe that he made a commitment to God. He did not ask the Lord for anything in return, but he gave freely and willingly the tithe that he believed belonged to God.

A few weeks later the college student, who had been faithful in his commitment, found that he was not short on any bills and he even had food to eat. He was amazed at how resourceful God is. And to top it all off, God blessed him with an unexpected gift that was more than ten times what he had given. Naturally, he was thoroughly convinced that when God tells us to tithe, He means it.

Tithing is not an option for the Christian, it is a blessing. Anon

Father, help us to give to You, what is already Yours. Amen

"Bring the whole tithe into the storehouse, so that there may be food in My house, and test Me now in this," says the Lord of hosts, if I will not open for you the windows of heaven, and pour out for you a blessing until it overflows."

Malachi 3:10
NASB

Just Weights

A group of teenage boys decided they were bored so they took some pellet guns and started shooting out street lights and shot holes in mail boxes. They were caught in the act and brought before a judge. They had no previous record, and they all came from good families who were present to support their sons. The judge believed them when they offered their apologies and promised to never do anything so foolish again. Even though he believed them and knew their parents were going to deal with them at home, he had a responsibility to those citizens whose property was damaged and destroyed. The judge imposed community service and made certain the boys worked off the debt. The boys learned from this experience and never got into trouble again.

The boys sin was pointed out to them in the court room and they confessed. The sin was forgiven, but there had to be restoration. Some of our confessed sin results in punishment.

heart of mercy...

When suffering for our sins, we can trust God to do what is best and just for us and for all involved. Gods punishment for sin shows His hatred for sin.

After we sin, God does something and He expects us to do something. He works in our hearts to convict us of our sin, and we are to confess and repent. He holds us accountable and, we are to take responsibility.

The pearl of justice is found in the heart of mercy. -- St. Catherine of Sinea

Father, God, You are a god of justice. Help us to love Your ways which are pure and right. Amen

But when we are judged, we are disciplined by the Lord in order that we may not be condemned along with the world.

I Corinthians 2:32 NASB

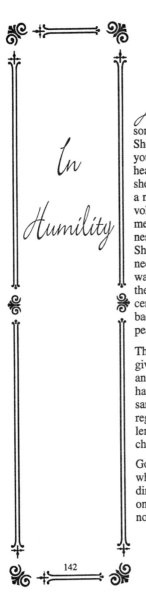

In Humility

peanut butter and

A wonderful Bible teacher had learned some valuable lessons in her sixty plus years. She taught a weekly Bible study to a group of young mothers. In humility, she opened her heart to these women. She told of how, when she was a young mother, every time there was a need in the church she was the first one to volunteer her help. When a family needed a meal delivered to them because of some illness, the birth of a child, etc., she responded. She spent hours preparing meals for the needy family and made certain everything was pleasing to the eye. She would drive to their home and help set the table and make certain things were perfect for them. Once back at her house she often served her family peanut butter and jelly sandwiches.

This saint had realized that it is important to give, to help those in need, but she was a wife and mother. On a rare occasion it might not have created a problem for her family to eat a sandwich for dinner, but this had become a regular occurrence that was creating problems in her own home with her husband and children.

God convicted her and she began to seek Him when a need arose. She allowed the Lord to direct her paths and by doing so, she was, once again, the peacemaker in her home -- not the instigator of discord.

jelly sandwiches

The Lord wants us to bless those in need. We are to be aware of the poor and needy and we are, most certainly, supposed to give. But, when we act out of pride and want to show those around us how good we are at what we do, we diminish the cause of Christ. Those we love and those that depend on us are often wounded in the process.

This dear one was able to help young wives and mothers to learn to listen to God and follow His will for them. She also helped them to see that it is okay to say no and then to not allow the enemy to come in and make us feel guilty because we did. She taught these young mothers that there is a time and a place for us to serve, and there is a time and a place for others to serve, as well.

Hard work is a thrill and joy when you are in the will of God.
– Robert A. Cook

Dear Savior and Lord, You are a God of order. Help us to listen to Your instruction about who we are to serve, when we are to serve, how we are to serve. Help us to not listen take on any condemnation from others if we have to say no. You know our hearts. Bless us, we pray. Amen

Humble yourself in the presence of the Lord, and He will exalt you.

James 4:10
NASB

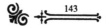

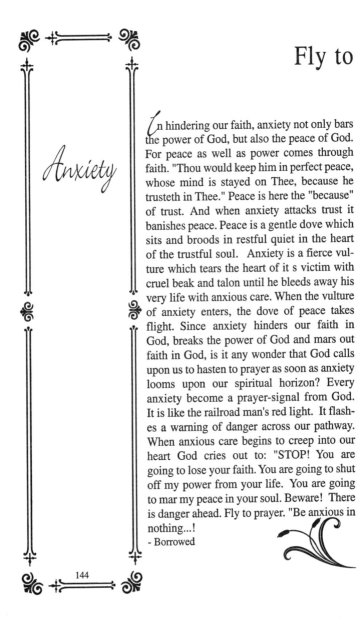

Fly to

Anxiety

In hindering our faith, anxiety not only bars the power of God, but also the peace of God. For peace as well as power comes through faith. "Thou would keep him in perfect peace, whose mind is stayed on Thee, because he trusteth in Thee." Peace is here the "because" of trust. And when anxiety attacks trust it banishes peace. Peace is a gentle dove which sits and broods in restful quiet in the heart of the trustful soul. Anxiety is a fierce vulture which tears the heart of it s victim with cruel beak and talon until he bleeds away his very life with anxious care. When the vulture of anxiety enters, the dove of peace takes flight. Since anxiety hinders our faith in God, breaks the power of God and mars out faith in God, is it any wonder that God calls upon us to hasten to prayer as soon as anxiety looms upon our spiritual horizon? Every anxiety become a prayer-signal from God. It is like the railroad man's red light. It flashes a warning of danger across our pathway. When anxious care begins to creep into our heart God cries out to: "STOP! You are going to lose your faith. You are going to shut off my power from your life. You are going to mar my peace in your soul. Beware! There is danger ahead. Fly to prayer. "Be anxious in nothing...!

- Borrowed

prayer....

Remember, you are destined for the throne! God is training you now. Your trials are not an accident: no suffering is purposeless. Your eternal profit is in view. Therefore, don't waste your sorrows! – Paul E. Billheimer

Father, our lives have so much in them that we tend to get anxious over the most mundane things. Lord, God, help us to run to You in prayer at the slightest impression of anxiety. Break us from allowing this enemy to rob us of our joy and position in You. Amen

Be anxious for nothing, but in everything by prayer and supplication with thanksgiving let your request be made known to God.

Philippians 4:6
NASB

Miracle Home

The young couple wanted to purchase a home, but knew they were in no position financially to do so. They did, however, know that if God wanted them to make the purchase He would make a way. They prayed and sought the Lord and an unexpected transfer offer came that meant a move to a new part of the state. They contacted a Real Estate Agent and began looking for a home. Interestingly, they had no down payment and no credit history. They were blessed with a Christian agent and they had many praying for them. They were excepted for a 100% loan and moved into the house before closing. Two weeks later, the agent called to say the loan fell through, but she had taken it to the senior Broker of her company and he had sent one of his best negotiators to the main office of FHA in the state to appeal the decision. He also sent word that FHA was back logged by months and just getting in the door would be a miracle. The couple took that to mean that they needed to call on Christian friends to pray that God would make that miracle happen.

Two hours after that call the Broker showed up at the door of the couple with the most amazing look on his face. As he sat down he began to shake his head and smile. He said, "I'm not the same denomination you are, but today I witnessed a miracle take place. When our negotiator went to the FHA office it was to try to set up an appointment to see someone in hopes that we could arrange for more time to work on a new loan so you

ashamed!

would not be forced to move. When she arrived she was pacing the hall like a hundred others waiting to see someone when a man called her into an office. The man was an old friend of her parents. He used to attend her fathers church ... her father is a minister. He asked what she was doing there she told him about you and said you are Christians and you really need this house and explained that the loan did not go through. He ask her if you would be good for the loan and she said you would so he took the file and approved the loan. The closing date is ....!" At that there was much praising God for not only had He performed a miracle by providing a home for the young couple, but a testimony of who He is was witnessed by many people that day. For years that Real Estate Broker told clients of how God performed a miracle right before his eyes. His agency continued to produce sales and became one of the most profitable businesses in the area. It did not matter that he was not a member of the same denomination as the young couple, He was not ashamed of what Christ had done.

God crosses over and through barriers all the time to perform His mighty miracles. Anon

God, You are performing miracles everyday. Open our hearts and eyes so we can recognize them and bear witness to others of Your great works. Amen

Cast not away therefore your confidence, which hath great recompense of reward. The eyes of all wait upon thee; and thou givest them their meat in due season. Thou openest thine hand, and satisfiest the desire of every living thing.

Psalm 145:15,16 KJV

Out of the

Convicted

His wife called to him while he was right in the middle of mowing the lawn in the hot Nevada sun. She needed laundry detergent right away and wanted him to drive down to the local connivance store to pick some up for her. He stopped what he was doing and he and his young son were off to the store. The man was a new Christian who had given up a lot of old habits when he came to know Christ.

Once in the store the man purchased the laundry soap for his wife and was leaving the store when he noticed some iced cold beer, which was very appealing after a long morning of mowing. The beer was 98 cents and he was short a few cents. He looked down at his son and asked him for the few pennies he needed to make his purchase. His little boy looked up at his daddy and with trembling voice said, "No, don't take my money to buy beer!" The man was speechless as he looked around at, what seemed like 2000 people, shaking their heads in disgust that a man would take his sons money to buy beer.

mouths of babes...

The man was so convicted has not drank in the forty years since and he never forgot that it was his son that reinforced what God was teaching him.

Out of the mouths of babes ... comes power that can convict! Anon

Lord, God, thank You for Your convicting power that helps keep us on the right path. Amen

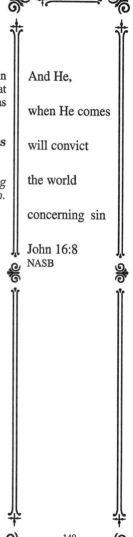

And He,

when He comes

will convict

the world

concerning sin

John 16:8
NASB

Play

Money

Real

My young sons helped me with the grocery shopping and they brought the bags in to the house for me. For that I let them have the S&H Green Stamps, but they had to accumulate them all year. At the beginning of each summer I made certain they had the latest Redemption book. They would sit for long periods of time looking at the book and counting their stamps. Then, it was a big deal the day we went to the S&H warehouse to redeem the stamps. Every year, without fail, they would have their minds made up, but once they entered that huge building lined with exciting boy things, they would change their minds a dozen times before finally deciding on one thing they would share. That was the beginning of helping them to understand the value of money and how to save and shop wisely. Each year I watched them as they made smarter choices than the year before.

the world...

There is so much for us to learn in this life. God, though, does not hand it all over to us at once, just like I would not have given my sons a pocket full of money to spend. We are so blessed to have a Parent, Father God, who knows just how much to put before us and just when to add the next lesson. There are levels of learning.

Corrie Ten Boom learned the same lesson when traveling with her father and she asked him for information that he felt she was too young to handle. He explained that there is a time to know certain things, and that time will be when we are wise enough to know what to do with the information.

A Godly man prefers grace before goods, and wisdom before the world.
– Richard Bernard

Jesus, I want to learn how to be wise. Please teach me at Your pace. Amen

... laying hold of the hope set before us. This hope we have as an anchor of the soul, a hope both sure and steadfast and one which enters within the veil.

Hebrews 6:18-19 NASB

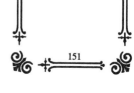

My Yoke Is Easy

*F*armers know the importance of yokes. A yoke is placed over the neck of two work animals to guarantee they are moving together as they pull a plow or a heavy load. The yoke might be hand crafted from the finest wood and metal and stained with the most beautiful satin finish. None of that matters unless the animals wearing the yoke are about the same size. If one is much larger than the other the yokes weight rest too heavily upon the shoulders of the smaller animal. When this happens, the animals aren't able to plow an even row and the smaller one wears out because he cannot shoulder the extra weight of the load.

Every relationship we have comes with an invisible yoke. If one person in the relationship is bearing the biggest part of responsibility then the relationship begins to crumble under the burden to that one. Even when little children are learning to pick up their rooms, sharing in that chore teaches them to carry part of the load in relationships. Lessons learned while toddlers carry over to adult relationships.

the Savior asks....

I heard a man say recently that he wished someone would teach his adult child to pick up behind himself. That lesson should have been learned many years ago. It is, however, never too late and we can all begin by picking up the pieces in relationships and shouldering our load.

God wants us to be actively involved in His work here on earth. To do that we must be prepared and willing to carry the truth to those around us.

We need each other as we serve the Lord, With all the workers equal to their tasks, No matter if the jobs are large or small, For faithfulness is all the Savior asks. – Hess

Father, in all relationships help us to be willing to carry our part of the load. Amen

Bear ye one

another's

burdens ...

Galatians 6:2
NASB

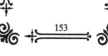

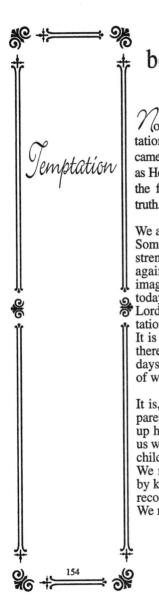

be strong and stand

Temptation

No one on earth has experienced temptation the way Christ was when Satan came to Him in the Garden of Gethsemane as He prayed. Jesus was able to send back the forces of evil because He knew the truth.

We are faced with temptations everyday. Some are so great it takes every bit of strength we can muster up to stand against the enemy. Adults can only imagine how difficult it must be for today's teenagers to be "strong in the Lord" when every where they turn temptations are of monumental proportions. It is nothing like when we parents were there age. Way back then, in the olden days, we had no clue about the majority of what our kids are faced with today.

It is, though, the responsibility of every parent to be aware of what the enemy has up his dirty old sleeve to temp not only us with, but what his schemes are for our children. There is no place sacred today. We must stand in the gap in prayer and by knowing the Word of God so we will recognize temptations, but also be there! We need to make our presence

against them

known as Godly parents and leaders. Author and international speaker, Dean Sherman, says, in his book Spiritual Warfare for Every Christian, that, "When we recognize the schemes of the enemy, they fail. Just recognizing them brings us victory. He preys on our ignorance and our weakness, but fails when confronted by our strength and knowledge of his schemes."

Temptations, when we meet them at first, are as the lion that reared upon Samson; but if we overcome them, the next time we see them we shall find a nest of honey within them. – *John Bunyan*

Jesus, we recognize that temptations will always be a part of life here. Help us, we pray, to know the schemes of the enemy so we can be strong and stand against them. Amen

No temptation has overtaken you but such as is common to man; and God is faithful, who will not allow you to be tempted beyond what you are able, but with the temptation will provide the way of escape also, that you may be able to endure it.

I Corinthians 10:13 NASB

Right

Of

Passage

*T*he move to another town was upsetting to the whole family, but particularly to one child. For her it was more than leaving her friends, church, and school behind. In her mind it was a Right of Passage from childhood to adulthood. As moving day approached she felt she had to make a decision that would impact her for ever. Her dolls were dear to her and she played with them every day and always slept with them by her side. They were gingerly propped up on her bed when she was not at home. She loved them with her whole heart.

In her mind, she could not have her dolls since she was growing up and moving away. She needed to be a BIG girl now. So, as the movers loaded the truck, she went to the side of the house and buried her dolls. It was a solemn moment and one her family did not know about until they had settled into their new home many miles away.

We all experience a Right of Passage although we may not call it that. We move from childhood into adulthood at different ages of our lives and in a variety of ways. We know some who are very mature about life as they make that transformation and there are others that we wonder if they will ever grow up.

the world...

The Lord tells us that we behaved like children when we were young, but as adults we need to act the part. There is a time to stop drinking babies formula and start taking in solid food. The analogy is that we stop acting like the world and take on the appearance of Christ when we become a Christian. Once we are born again there is a continuos progression of growth and final maturity comes when we enter the presence of God the Father in heaven.

...do not be conformed to this world, but be transformed by the renewing of your mind,that you may prove what the will of God is, that which is good and acceptable and perfect.
– Paul

Lord, Jesus, I pray that the growth will continue to move at a steady pace as I study Your Word and learn to be Christlike. Amen

..like newborn

babes,

long for the

pure milk

of the word,

that by it you

may grow in

respect to

salvation...

I Peter 2:2
NASB

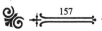